WOW MOMENTS!

Turning Everyday Experiences into Extraordinary Events

By

Mark D. Kent

Content

Dedication

Chapters

1. Leaving The World A Better Place
2. A Wow Moment Culture
3. A Wow Moment Reaction
4. Exceeding Expectations
5. Where The Magic Happens
6. Defining Success (And Moving Beyond It)
7. A Wow Moment Environment
8. A Wow Moment Buy-in
9. Success And The Wow Moment
10. The Wow In Accountability
11. Innovation And The Wow Moment
12. Communication And The Wow Moment
13. Vision, Values, And Wow Moment Characteristics
14. Wow Moment Outcomes
15. It's All About Promoting Action
16. One Shoe Does Not Fit All
17. Wow Moments Leave Nothing To Chance
18. Honoring The Past To Affect The Future
19. Improvisation And The Wow Moment
20. Attitude And The Wow Moment
21. Wow Moments And The Power Of Emotional Engagement
22. The Personal Connection
23. Customers For Life
24. Acquisition, Growth And The Wow Moment Culture
25. The Wow Moment Culture

© Copyright protected material for Kent Publishing

Registered owner: WOW MOMENTS!™

Dedication:

This book is dedicated to my family who unconditionally believes that I can do anything they direct me to do!

I love you very much.

CHAPTER ONE

Leaving the World a Better Place

What is a Wow Moment?

A Wow Moment makes an experience extraordinary. A Wow Moment takes what we expect from a situation, event, or interaction and elevates it to the unexpected. A Wow Moment provides an unanticipated, lasting spark to a relationship and creates a memorable experience.

While our primary focus in the pages to come will be to explore creating Wow Moments for your customers, clients, and associates – moments that elevate the stature of your business in their eyes – we will also explore Wow Moments that infuse meaning and wonder into our relationships, our community, and our world outside of work.

I've spent most of my career in the medical profession. I run medical centers. Providing an exceptional healthcare experience is the bottom line to everything I do; making that experience extraordinary in the eyes of our patients is what separates us from our competitors down the street, across town, and all the ones trying emulate our success. It will do the same for your business, regardless of your industry.

It was a Wow Moment that pointed me in the direction of the healthcare industry in the first place. I was 13 when I lost my grandmother. It was the most heartbreaking experience of my life. Grandma was the pillar of our family. She was the glue. Her name was Dorothy Kent, and I spent a large part of my childhood sharing her love and learning from her. Losing her was a Wow Moment that changed my life.

Grandma Kent died of diabetes. This was 30 years ago. Today it would never have happened. Advances in modern medicine and our understanding today of how diet and exercise help to manage diabetes might have given her another 25 years. But the education and the understanding we have today of such diseases didn't exist then. For a 13-year-old, it was devastating. All I wanted to do was save her in some way. It was this event, as negative as it may have been, that sparked my interest in healthcare, a spark that has never died. Her death and the disease that killed her were the impetus and the catalyst for who I am today.

Wow Moments come in all shapes and sizes. As you can see from my experience with my Grandma, not all of them are pleasant. Some are painful. Some are inspiring. Some are life changing. Some just make for a better day.

Educating patients so they have a better understanding of their disease is a huge part of what we do in my medical centers every day. Back in my grandmother's day, for example, we didn't know how significant diet and exercise were in the life of a diabetic. Now we can explain the cause and effect of the choices they make and help them to make the right choices for a healthier life.

I began my career working in direct patient care as a registered nurse, but I also studied business because I knew early on that I wanted to have more control over the administration of healthcare. The Wow Moment for me in this respect was not that accountants, lawyers, and C-level managers ran most clinics, nursing homes, and hospitals, but that these people actually had no experience in truly touching a patient. They had no understanding of what motivates the men, women, or children in their care or how their behaviors influence health. Most importantly, they had no clue as to how to fundamentally assist and help the people being treated in their facilities.

That was the Wow Moment that made me realize how much greater my impact could be if I combined a knowledge of patient care with an understanding of the business of healthcare. Instead of impacting one person at a time, I could actually impact hundreds if not thousands of people towards bettering their lives.

Two generations ago my family came to the United States via Jamaica. Our journey took us through Florida to New York and finally to Indiana. Education was the number one priority in our family. The message I got from both my grandparents and my parents was simple: the best way to a better life is through education. If you keep pushing, you can always get better, and the moment you're satisfied is the moment you stop growing.

There's always an opportunity to get better. There is always an occasion, as my Grandma liked to say, to advance the ball down the field.

There are no age limits on Wow Moments. Age has no bearing on creating Wow Moments or experiencing them. I remember coming home from school one day complaining about how much I hated my teacher and how sick I was of homework; I figured my Grandma to be the perfect person with whom to air these complaints. In one sense, this proved to be true. But instead of sympathizing, she pulled me aside and gave me some of the best advice I was ever to hear. She said, "Mark, every day that the sun rises and sets and you haven't done something to move the ball forward for yourself or your family or your community, then you've wasted that day."

I was 10 years old, and I will never forget the absolutely sincere look on her face. And I never forgot her words either. They became a fundamental part of my core being. I believe that we're here to leave the world better than we found it, and I've told my own son this a hundred times.

WOW Moments can work in mysterious ways and come from the most unexpected sources.

I remember how moved I was when I heard the story of a 4-year-old foster child named Rilya Wilson. Rilya went missing while living in the home of her caretaker here in Florida. Her disappearance went unnoticed by the state for nearly two years, and she was never found.

The incident left such an indelible impression on me that I began researching the foster care system in Florida and found that the state was charged with the care and oversight of more than 4,000 children, a near impossible task. What I found was that most lived at or below the poverty line and that their educational prospects were dire at best. This was the same system that had so thoroughly failed Rilya Wilson.

I knew I couldn't stand by and do nothing, so I created a not-for-profit foundation called FOCUS Foundation for Foster Children. The foundation's aim was to provide backpacks and school supplies for as many of these foster kids as we could. Our first year we reached out to more than 400 children and made certain they had the supplies they needed to face the school day. It was a good start. I remember what moved me the most was the overwhelming reaction these small contributions produced: a grateful smile on a child's face; a look of gratitude in a school coordinator's eyes when we delivered a load of backpacks; a hug and a thank you from a foster mom.

Still, I knew we could do more.

Yet the more I got involved, the more I realized that neither the local foster families taking in these kids, as big as their hearts may have been, nor the state had enough resources to deal with the crisis.

Many times I would go home angry and mentally exhausted. The roadblocks and obstacles standing in the way of changing a situation society had created and allowed to fester was daunting.

The turning point for me – my personal WOW Moment – occurred one rainy afternoon as I was driving home after a long day.

I pulled up to a red light and caught sight of a teenaged girl sitting at a bus stop rocking back and forth and looking completely lost. I rolled down my window and asked her if she needed help. She shook her head "no," but I could see that she was crying and shaking from the cold. I pulled over and got out. I crouched down next to her and asked again what I could do for her. Was there someplace I could take her? Someone I could call? Sarah, not her real name, could barely respond through the tears. When I offered to call the police, she said that wouldn't help. Then she dried her eyes and looked me. She said, "I'm just so tired of trying. Life just seems so unfair."

She told me how she'd been accepted to a local college but couldn't afford it. She'd been living in foster homes her entire life, but now that she was 18, there were no longer benefits or assistance available. She was homeless.

Amazingly, my phone rang at that very moment. Call it providence if you will, but it was a mother from one of the foster families I'd visited that day calling to thank me for the supplies I'd provided for her children. Not one to ignore the hand of fate, I told her about the young lady and asked if I might bring her by. The foster mother agreed. When we arrived, the foster mother told that there were, in fact, no transitional services available for foster kids aging out of the system.

I went home that evening determined to help this young lady. Here was someone trying to positively impact her own life and couldn't seem to catch a break. It wasn't right. How could I help? There had to be a way.

I woke up the next morning with an idea that, if done right, would expand the scope of our foundation and provide scholarships for foster children who had been accepted to colleges, universities, and trade schools in the Florida area. I enlisted the help of friends and donors, and our first scholarship was awarded less than six months later. The recipient? You guessed it. The very young lady I had met that rainy day. As I write this today, she is a college graduate who recently graduated from law school and aspires to be a judge someday.

Yes, our charity still provides backpacks and schools supplies to foster kids throughout Florida, but it also provides scholarships and transition services to assist young adults aging out of the system and facing the uncertainty of life on their own.

———

All life is made of experiences. It is when we determine to make those experiences into extraordinary events that we enter the world of WOW Moments.

———

CHAPTER TWO

A WOW Moment Culture

I come by my dual interest in healthcare and business naturally. My father was a family physician. My mother was an attorney practicing patent law and general counsel. Aided by my grandmother's counsel, insight and strong Christian values, my parents raised me to believe that it was our obligation as human beings to make a difference in the world.

That attitude may have contributed to my workaholic tendencies, but, more importantly, it contributed to a life philosophy of going the extra mile for the people in your life, both at work and at home. At work, this means raising the level of your customer involvement beyond the normal experience. It means offering services that not only supersede the basics, but also moves even the most ordinary experience toward something memorable and exceptional. That's the WOW Moment we're talking about.

Business came naturally for me. My dad would pay me ten dollars to mow the grass. I'd pay the kid down the street six dollars to do it and pocket the other four. We both came out ahead; that is until my dad found out.

I went to college prepared to study medicine. It was my dad who encouraged me to follow my love of business as well, which translated into double majors in nursing and business.

Right out of college, a good buddy and I started a recruiting company with a focus on the IT industry. Joe was an IT specialist. My strength was making connections and networking. We called our company Network Connections Group. I hadn't yet established the premise behind the WOW Moment concept, but I did know that we had to stand out in a market crowded with IT people. The recruiting business required two components: the companies in need of qualified IT people, and the right people to fill the positions. The first contract I negotiated was with Enterprise Rent-A-Car. They had jobs in the IT area that needed qualified people, and we found them people who fulfilled their expectations and more. The WOW Moment for Enterprise Rent-A-Car came with the realization that our company wasn't just pulling names out of a hat, but finding people willing to go above and beyond for their company. That relationship led to contracts with the likes of IBM Global and

Anheuser Busch. In just three years, we became one of the top 20 IT recruiting companies in the business. We grew from three employees to 117 and were making money hand over fist.

Being young and foolish, Joe and I sold the company after three years to the number one consulting company in our field, a group who desperately wanted the contracts we had.

Despite my youth and impetuous nature back then, those three years were ripe with learning experiences and provided me with an unspoken foundation for the WOW Moment business philosophy that we're now discussing.

Intuitively, I knew even back then that in everything we do as human beings, we are looking for relationships and connections. We may be solitary beings from a physical standpoint, but it is in our nature to build bridges.

The question I always ask is this: How can I identify with you, or anyone else, as a person? From a business perspective, the question is similar: How can I identify with you as a customer, as an associate, as a fellow worker? And in the healthcare field more specifically, how can I identify with you as a patient? So whether black or white, young or old, man or woman, we are all looking to identify with one another in our communications, our interactions, and our relationships. In business, in particular, this makes the ability to network and connect critically important.

The root of this skill comes from a foundation of caring. For some of us, this comes naturally. For others, it must be learned and cultivated. In any case, this foundation of genuinely caring about people leads, without question, to a desire to interact on a positive level. It fosters active problem solving, which is of unquestionable importance in the art of relationships. It also fosters a desire to get better, to be better, and to offer something above and beyond the average experience.

In the recruiting business, this foundation of caring translated, perhaps unconsciously at the time, into a desire to discover the root cause of our clients' needs. What were their issues? What were they truly looking for in terms of quality, long-term employees? How could I drill down to the heart and soul of their expectations and deliver something even better? I believed that if I could do this, I would, essentially, have a client for life. Who could ask more than that?

No, I wasn't yet calling the delivery of this exceptional interaction a WOW Moment. But I did see it as a foundation of service. I was focusing on how our company could service clients' needs by helping them identify and define what success was, and then providing something extra.

———

The WOW Moment then is the extra on top of what they see as success.

———

In the sales world, they call the needs of the client identifying the "pain." The man or woman who is particularly good at this process is, first, inquisitive by nature, and second, is a person who listens far more than he or she talks, and third, whose goal is a genuine understanding of a client's needs.

———

The more you understand, the better you can connect. The better you connect, the more viable the solution.

———

My Grandma, for example, had a natural way of connecting with people. She had a natural way of hearing the true meaning of their words and of offering salient advice without ever sounding condescending. She had no formal education to speak of, yet what she did have was that ability to truly and fundamentally connect. She never made another person feel defensive. She never second-guessed. Whoever she was talking to, despite their age, their gender, or their beliefs, saw her as caring and understanding.

In the workplace these are truly indispensable traits. If you're genuine about connecting, your superiors, your peers, and your subordinates immediately see you as credible. Even more importantly, your clients, your customers, and your contacts see you as credible.

The bottom line is this: When someone sees you as caring and understanding, he'll naturally open up to you. It's the way humans are made. We all look for ways to connect. It's up to each one of us to make the most of this human quality.

We all have a series of filters when we're dealing with other people, in particular in the workplace. These filters allow us to make decisions about another person's character, motives, and authenticity. If our filters identify a person who is unresponsive or lacks caring, we move on, and we move on quickly.

The patients populating our medical centers are perfect examples. A staff member who takes the time to say, "Hello, how are you?" meets our 'service basic.' All well and good. A staff member who remembers the names of a patient's kids and inquires about their soccer game, has now created a meaningful experience for a patient. A staff member who attends one of those soccer games has connected on an extraordinary level and created a WOW Moment.

In my IT recruiting company, it was just as important for me to create a relationship with the HR managers at our client firms as with the men and women we were recruiting for the firm. So, for example, if I knew that the HR manager at XYZ Company loved dogs and I discovered that one of our potential recruits was an animal lover as well, I would have been more likely to bring the two together, knowing such common ground is often the makings of a good relationship.

In any case, you have to test a person's sincerity, one, because bona fide connections are built upon honesty and and authenticity, and two, because a lack of sincerity is easy to unmask.

I was 26 when I sold Network Connections Group, and it was, ironically, a WOW Moment of a different kind that precipitated the sale. It wasn't that the offer was one we just couldn't refuse. And it wasn't that I was dying to find something else to do. It was fear. It wasn't a fear of success, and it wasn't a fear of failure. We were already wildly successful for such a young company. We had nearly 120 employees, and it was a comment by one of those employees that ignited the fear. I can remember it like it was yesterday. It was a Friday night, and a group of us had gathered at a local watering hole for cocktails. I happened to be standing at the bar when one of my best recruiters, a guy in his mid-thirties, came up and began thanking me in the most glowing terms for all I'd done for him.

"My wife and I can finally buy the house we've been dreaming about thanks to you, and we're putting our daughter in a private school," he said. "I can't thank you enough."

Obviously, this could have been an inspiring WOW Moment.

Here I was providing an opportunity for this man. He was on a good career path. He was making good money. He was planning for his future. It wasn't until I got home that night that the fear hit me like a sucker punch.

I replayed our conversation word for word, and the implications scared me. It scared me because here was this man's future staring me in the face, and I was responsible for it. His job was providing for a wife, a home, a mortgage. It was the source of the tuition for his daughter's school. All on me. A business that up to now I had treated with a somewhat cavalier attitude suddenly became very, very real.

That conversation changed everything. I woke up in a cold sweat at three in the morning. I started seeing the business differently from that moment forward. I started seeing our people differently. I started seeing their families and their futures. I realized how much I cared for these people, and it wasn't as much fun suddenly. I got scared.

Seven months later, my partner and I were approached for the second time in six months by the same consulting company, and this time we said yes to their offer, an undervalued offer at that.

So sometimes WOW Moments have an unintended effect. A moment that should have energized and inspired me caused me to spend too much time second-guessing myself and the future of my business. In retrospect, however, the very same moment served as a fabulous learning tool. I came away from it smarter and stronger. I came away from it understanding myself better as a leader. I came away from it knowing I wanted to reach out to people, especially young people, and offer experience and knowledge that might potentially lead them to take some positive action or to believe in themselves a bit more than they may have previously. So, in the end, the WOW Moment was very positive.

―――

When you make a genuine connection, one that comes from a place of caring and concern, then both parties are more apt to open up and relate to one another.

―――

It is that very fundamental level of connection that allows you to get to the WOW Moment. You create an environment where the person sitting across from you is no longer guarded. And in the ebb and flow of this interaction, the person tells you what success looks like in his eyes. And more importantly, he also tells you where the WOW is for him.

CHAPTER THREE

A WOW Moment Reaction

As a parent, it's very exciting when your child comes home from school with good grades; good grades are an expectation in our house, but I'm still proud when Corey shows his commitment to the standards we've set for him. This is the ground floor, if you will. The foundation. I am, however, very "wowed" when he comes home with exceptional grades AND has been spending time on his weekends with Habitat for Humanity. Reaching out with a helping hand that way, and doing so without needing credit or recognition for what he's done, is his way of getting me to the WOW.

Coming home with straight As is good and that's certainly success in my eyes, but his unselfish community work takes the experience to the extraordinary. As a father and a businessman, I have taken the time to share this concept of the WOW Moment with him, and he understands how much it means to me as the recipient. He also understands, however, how much he gets in return from the act of delivering a WOW Moment. It is very much a two-way street.

Now that the concept of the WOW Moment has been introduced into my medical centers, I see how our staff members have embraced it. They see that making an experience extraordinary for our patients adds to the value of the job they are doing and the sense of self-worth they get in creating these special moments.

I think back and realize how much I had to learn after my grandmother's death, and how little understanding I had about the effect we can have upon one another. After her death, I was angry, pure and simple. And not just for a few weeks or a few months; I carried this debilitating anger around with me for a number of years. In fact, I fully mourned her until I was 21.

This anger might have gotten the best of me had it not been for the scoutmaster of my Boy Scout Troop. His name was Mr. Kowalski, and he understood where this extremely powerful emotion was coming from. He also understood how destructive it could be if something wasn't done.

He stepped in. He said, "Moving forward after a loss like that takes discipline. It takes focus."

He told me about the loss of his own grandfather and gave me a glimpse into the grief this caused him. I was genuinely moved by this act of sharing, and it gave me permission to open up to him in return. Mr. Kowalski didn't judge me; he empathized. What he didn't do was sympathize. He said, "I understand what you're going through, and I know it's hard, but life goes on. Your obligation to your grandmother now is to start living your life and to move ahead. That takes discipline and courage, but that's what life is all about."

My middle school teacher, Mr. Johnston, who was equally as instrumental in my early years, took a different approach. He called me out. He said, "You're too smart for this kind of behavior. Sure you're angry. But you've got to let it go and here's why. Society doesn't owe you anything. Society didn't take your grandma. Her poor health did. So you've got to get past it. Otherwise you're destined for a very long and very hard life."

Every day after school, Mr. Johnston took a few minutes out of his day to talk to me. He did this for months. It became a part of our routine, and I began to look forward to it. Sometimes we'd talk about the school day. Sometimes we'd just talk about life. But always with an eye on the future. Our connection wasn't emotional; it was more like a drill sergeant and one of his charges. He didn't let me get bored in school. He pushed me at every turn. If I was reading at a seventh grade level, he would push me to the eighth grade level. If I was doing algebra in math, he pushed me into geometry and calculus. He would look me right in the eye and say, "I see the kid your grandmother saw. I see the kid she raised. Time to start acting like it."

Mr. Kowalski and Mr. Johnston. Two men who were as genuine as they were sincere. Back to back WOW Moments.

I learned life-changing lessons from them. Without sincerity and authenticity, you won't go far. Going through the motions is not an option, not if you want to build something that's lasting or meaningful. In looking back now, I realize how important these two men – a scoutmaster and a middle school teacher – were in forging my decisions moving forward.

I learned that showing your true self and allowing yourself to be vulnerable are at the heart of a true connection and fundamental to creating WOW Moments.

You have to be willing to give of yourself. You also have to be willing to receive, which can be just as scary.

One thing is certain: People want to connect. It's human nature. We all seek interpersonal relationships founded in trust and honesty. Interpersonal relationships are not, however, based upon one person mirroring another. It's not about suggesting that someone take a page out of your book or vice versa. It's not a matter of "Look at me. I'm happy. And you can be happy too." It's about respecting others' views of the world. It's about acknowledging where they are in their life and being genuine about your interest in their situation.

Whether we're talking about business relationships or those outside the workplace, a WOW Moment goes beyond the expected.

If it's expected, then it's not a WOW. Yes, delivering the expected can and should be viewed as a success. Giving a client, customer, or, in my world, a patient exactly what he or she expects, does in fact constitute a success. When patients enter one of our medical centers, they know they are going to get quality service. They expect it, and rightfully so.

When we visit our local Starbucks, the people behind the counter are going to give us a hot cup of coffee and it's going to taste good. That's expected. What's not expected is a barista who remembers your name and already has your order in the queue before you even get to the counter. That's a WOW Moment.

In our business, it's an RN who stops in the middle of his or her busy day to ask a patient if she'd feel a little more comfortable if someone brought her a hot cup of coffee while she waits. It's more than service; it's caring. When I go into Starbucks, I'm expecting good service. I'm not expecting someone to reach out and try to connect, and that's special. That's the experience taken to the WOW, and that's extremely good business whether you're brewing coffee or treating sick people.

Let's look at it from another perspective. I think we can safely say that most personal connections are emotionally based. Emotions and behaviors are fundamentally joined, and our behaviors are predicated, most often, upon an emotional reaction.

WOW Moments send a positive message to the brain, but they also send a positive message to the heart.

That's why they feel so good.

People remember WOW Moments because they trigger positive reactions from both the head and the heart, and that's good for business. It's also good for a marriage, a friendship, or a casual acquaintance.

The brain stores memories, and the strongest memories are emotional. Our brains know when someone has gone the extra mile for us, and it triggers an appropriate reaction, one which is almost always sincere, grateful, and excited.

When I'm teaching the WOW Moment concept to my team, I make it very clear that you get as much as you give. This is also human nature. It's why we like to give at Christmas as much as we like to receive. As human beings, going the extra mile to elevate an experience or an expectation to the level of a WOW is just as rewarding for the provider as it is for the recipient. I want the giving of WOW Moments to our patients to become a habit for my staff, and knowing the satisfaction they'll feel in return makes this all the more likely.

After I sold Network Connections Group I moved to Florida, more or less on a whim. Shortly thereafter, I began consulting with a start-up company called Spectra Care. Their business model was based upon providing home-based healthcare and in-home healthcare specialists.

When Spectra Care began, their clients were generally the patients themselves or the families of the patients. This working arrangement was called self-pay. The problem with the self-pay model was lack of sustainability; once the patient no longer needed the company's services, that income stream disappeared.

My job was to ease Spectra Care out of the self-pay market and to build a clientele of insurance companies such as United Healthcare, Aetna, or Humana. The insurance companies would then provide a steady stream of patients requiring home healthcare, but Spectra Care would bill the companies, not the patients. My job was to convince the insurance companies that Spectra Care deserved a place on their home healthcare rosters. Not easy. Who needs one more name on their home healthcare roster? And if Humana or Aetna or whoever has 32 home healthcare providers on its list and Spectra Care is thirty-second on the list, it doesn't matter because people almost always select from the top five names.

So my task was twofold. One, get Spectra Care on the provider list, and two, break through the clutter to the top spot. I knew two things: I would have to build a relationship with the right people, and I would have to create a meaningful connection. So the question was, who were the right people?

To begin with, I targeted Humana, AvMed, and Vista. And I knew it was more than just getting on the list. That was easy. Getting results required us to make an impact on the people making healthcare recommendations to the patients. There were two possible strategies: push or pull. Insurance companies might "pull" us onto their lists, but then no one would be recommending us. Or, I could get doctors and physician groups – the people who actually make the recommendations – to "push" us onto the provider lists. I chose this latter strategy, because I knew my success would be based upon making positive connections with individuals, not institutions. If I could convince these doctors and physician groups of the quality of Spectra Care's services, and also our ability to go beyond the service basics to exceptional experiences, then I was confident we would be on the right track.

This was the campaign I initiated, and I realized the key was not unlike the one I had adapted at Network Connections Group when we were recruiting IT personnel for companies such as IBM and Enterprise Rent-A-Car. Create relationships. Connect. Identify a need.

First, I researched the physician groups I wanted to target. Then I organized physician focus groups to identify their needs and their goals. Finally, I went for the WOW Moment by sitting with

35

physicians one-on-one. I didn't try to sell them on Spectra Care as much as I explored the problems they and their patients most often encountered with home healthcare. I explored what it would mean to them if a company went above and beyond the normal to ensure these problems were resolved. How would that look? Suddenly, I wasn't a salesman. I was a sounding board. Suddenly, I wasn't just offering a service package. I was offering to go the extra mile for them and their patients. I was suddenly an ally, a partner, a difference maker. We formed a connection. A relationship.

The referrals started to roll in. Suddenly their patients were coming back to them and saying, "Thank you for referring Spectra Care." "My nurse is so awesome." "I actually feel special."

The physicians became our primary means of advertising. They began "pushing" us onto provider lists and doing so gladly.

Some months later, I took an ownership position in Spectra Care. We moved from home health into home hemodialysis. The cattle-car experience of the typical dialysis center suddenly became a more respectable lifesaving procedure in the privacy of a patient's own home. It saved time, and it saved money. It provided dignity. Patients loved it, and physicians started recommending it. It was, in many ways, the ultimate WOW Moment for people who had been enduring the indignity and horrors of overcrowded dialysis centers. It meant one-on-one treatment in the comfort of their own beds by a nurse able to give them every ounce of her attention.

Like I do at my medical centers these days, we were recruiting nurses who understood the value of creating a meaningful connection with our patients. Yes, they were paid well, but they also understood the value of taking basic services to a higher level and pushing an experience into the realm of the extraordinary.

We identified the WOW not only for the physician recommending our services, but even more so for the patient who was now receiving treatment and care beyond his expectations.

CHAPTER FOUR

Exceeding Expectations

There is a very definite process that we teach at our medical centers for creating WOW Moments. It begins with a culture of service at the foundation. Everything we do focuses first and foremost on service. That is the expectation we want every one of our associates, from top to bottom, to embrace. It is also a culture we want every one of our patients – customers, if you will – to walk through the door expecting.

―――

When I think about this foundation, I believe that the higher your floor is the higher your ceiling will always be. Set your standards high and grow from there.

―――

The first step, therefore, is a very clearly defined expectation. Now we talk about moving beyond that expectation to a bona fide experience. When you create an experience, you begin with a very clear design. Looking back at Spectra Care's home healthcare program and our home hemodialysis service, for example, the design was based upon the vision that our patients themselves would have of that experience. We wanted them to go back to their primary physician saying, "Wow, these people are great. They provided an exceptional experience."

In the case of our Spectra Care process, the design began with face-to-face, personalized conversations with the patient and his or her family, and what we called a comprehensive needs assessment. In other words, creating a connection and building a relationship from the outset.

This series of personalized conversations formed the foundation of a checklist we called a Home Assessment. It covered everything from their last doctor appointments and any recent hospital visits to an evaluation of the drugs a patient might be taking. The job of our home healthcare nurses was to make sure the patients truly understood the meds they had been prescribed and why they were taking them. Part of this job was communicating with patients' primary physicians to make sure everyone was on the same page. We weren't just taking orders from the patient's doctor and showing up, which is what most homebound patients were accustomed to; we were creating a meaningful dialogue that demonstrated a genuine level of involvement.

An underlying and inherent aspect of the Spectra Care home assessment experience was a review of all safety issues, which, naturally, reinforced for the patients how much we cared about them. That's where the WOW Moment came in.

When the patient thinks, "This isn't just a job to this nurse. She really cares about my well-being," then you've made the experience extraordinary.

Simply creating an experience around the home assessment checklist and demonstrating a fundamental caring for the patient, moving well beyond the step-by-step process, created a new environment. The patient truly feels valued, and the caregiver feels a sense of fulfillment. That's a WOW Moment for them both. And finally, there is the primary care physician. He comes away from the experience thinking, "Here's an organization that really gets it and really cares, so I will keep referring my patients to them."

There is not a business or industry that doesn't face the same hurdle. Yours does. So does mine. It is a cliché perhaps to say that customer satisfaction is at the heart of all successful enterprises, but what so many business men and women don't realize and can't visualize is the power of taking what your customer expects and creating an experience exceptional enough to secure his loyalty as far into the future as you or I am willing to look.

I hire people blessed with a certain personality profile; the bottom line of that profile is a man or woman who gets the concept of the WOW Moment as an irreplaceable tool. Is the work that person is doing a calling or just a paycheck? Is it a career or a job? Healthcare, my particular industry, is a little easier, because most caregivers consider their work a calling. Not all. Every now and again you do find the guy who became a physician with an eye on the salary he could earn or the boat he could buy. Most, however, say, "I fundamentally care. I take good health very seriously and want to see my patients get better. I want to see them heal. I want to see them thrive."

Very much germane to this personality profile we're discussing is a person's ability to understand people and their needs.

It's not about checking a box. Said hello: *check*. Ask how they were doing: *check*. Put on a smile: *check*. If a person's interaction with clients or customers is based solely upon a checklist, you're in trouble.

―――

The hiring process at any level, no matter what the industry, is best served when individuals capable of creating positive customer experiences are brought into the fold.

―――

When I hire a nurse for one of our medical centers, I always want to know how she sees herself as a nurse (or in the case of a man, how he sees himself in this role). I want to know why she became a nurse. If she says, "Oh my God, I love it. There is something about touching a patient every day. There is something about being with them every day and watching them get better and heal. It's just magical. I really feel like God called me to this field," I know I'm onto something. Why? Because this person is demonstrating the qualities that it takes to make an experience extraordinary.

Certainly, the people you bring into your company have to match the requirements of the job in terms of qualifications, skills, and experience. We're not discounting this. But once those parameters are established, your next step is to drill down to find a person with the ability to connect and create relationships.

The bottom line is this: Not everyone has the ability to create WOW Moments.

In our business, it's the candidates that truly "see" the person they're treating. They don't just see a job with a job description and a list of chores. It's a calling. It's holistic and it's all encompassing.

Unless you're in a completely automated industry, the WOW Moment concept is applicable. Where there are humans, there is human interaction. Where there is human interaction, there are connections. And where there are connections, there are expectations. With expectations comes an opportunity to excel and to move beyond what is expected. That's when you begin creating an experience. That's when you open the door to a WOW Moment.

If you're an accountant who deals in numbers, there are still people behind those numbers. If you're a roofer, there are still people living under those roofs and the need for human-to-human interaction exists.

A smart accountant wants her clients to succeed. She wants them to enjoy the fruits of their efforts, so she doesn't just crunch numbers; that's the service basic that every client expects. She goes beyond that. She makes it an experience by explaining the numbers and providing an understanding of what the numbers mean. She offers financial advice where appropriate. Then she provides a WOW Moment by catering lunch for the client's entire office.

A roofing contractor doesn't just pound nails. He does more than just talk to the insurance company and pick up his check. He explains the nature of any problems a roof might have to his customer. Then he adds some extra flashing to a troublesome spot free of charge.

If you're in business, you have to be a people person to a certain degree. You need to know what a client's expectations are and take that step above and beyond. You need to become an advocate for your client's best interest.

If the accountant in our example has made a genuine effort to know her client at a personal level, then she might know that the client's goal is to pass his business on to his kids someday. What if she foresees a lack of profitability that might not allow this to happen or a long-term flaw in his business model? Now she's in a position to say, "Down the road, you may need another source of revenue or there is a very real chance the business won't be sustainable. Let's talk about what that might be."

One of the long-term effects of creating WOW Moments for your customers is that they will now see you as an ally, a person who gets where they're coming from and what their needs are. When the patients at our medical centers view us as an ally with their best interest at heart, they don't even think about alternative healthcare providers. They come to us because they see people who truly care.

WOW Moments occur when you exceed expectations.

WOW Moments occur when you demonstrate that you fundamentally understand. When you're at this stage in a relationship, it is actually the client or the customer who tells you what you'll need in order to create a WOW Moment. You don't have to guess. You look at the expected experience and take it up a notch. You go above and beyond. The additional payback is that this very client now becomes your net promoter in the community, and you can't buy better advertising than that.

A good referral, we all know, is like striking gold. So this type of relationship not only translates into loyalty, but also into additional revenue. And let's not kid ourselves into thinking that we can run our businesses on good will alone. We said it earlier: all people want to connect. The accountant and her client, the roofer and his customers, the staff at our medical centers and our patients. Everyone.

The key to every WOW Moment is authenticity, because authenticity is the key to all genuine connections. It can't be faked.

You know it's genuine when you go home and your efforts at work reflect positively on your relationships there. When you create WOW Moments in the workplace, the fallout is a more enjoyable experience outside of work. It comes back to you. It always comes back to you.

CHAPTER FIVE

Where the Magic Happens

When I was working as a nurse at St. John's Hospital in St. Louis, I was always extremely impressed to meet elderly couples who had been married for 40 or 50 or even 60 years. I always wanted to know their secret. What had sustained them all those years? The response that framed it the best for me came from an 81-year-old dialysis patient. She looked at me and smiled when I asked her that question. "I always took the chipped plate," she said.

Ironically, I asked her husband that very question, and his response was the same. "I always took the chipped plate." Their answers resonated with me in the most powerful way. They were both expressing the same sentiment: He always looked out for her, and she always looked out for him.

Their relationship came first. It superseded everything else.

In a certain way, "I always took the chipped plate" became a personal mantra when it came to building strong and lasting relationships, even if I didn't use those exact words.

The more we reach out, the more people and events we're able to affect in a positive way. And the more lives we affect, the more we grow as human beings.

As I described earlier, I applied some form of this people-to-people methodology in my ownership tenures with Network Connection Group and Spectra Care, and my son Corey brought this full circle for me in my personal life.

After I sold my ownership interest in Spectra Care to a group called Renal Care Partners, I accepted a position with Humana.

Humana offered a unique opportunity for me in the wake of selling two very successful businesses. When I consulted my dad about the opportunity, he cautioned me about the pitfalls of corporate America, especially in light of my recent successes as a small businessman. He felt strongly that I was meant to be an entrepreneur. How was I going to fit in? How was I going to respond to directives from people with more authority than me? His questions were legitimate.

I saw Humana's offer as an opportunity to build something special within the healthcare community, and on a larger scale than my previous ventures had allowed.

I also saw it as a challenge, as a chance to grow, and, as my grandmother liked to say, move the ball down the field. I was given the very nebulous title of project manager, which made a number of my friends laugh. They said, "You've owned two companies that were wildly successful, and now you're going into this other company as a project manager."

The title was the least of my concerns. It was the experience and the learning that compelled me. Very quickly, I began to rise through the ranks. One of the leadership traits that I felt separated me from many of the other executives in the corporate maelstrom was my view of the customer. I believed that our success or failure as a company was a direct result of the relationship we build with them.

Though at the time Humana was primarily an insurance company, and one of the largest in the world, they also owned a number of medical centers within the South Florida area. These centers were in need of reorganization as a strategic business unit. Because Humana had divested of most of the hospitals they had owned around the country, my job was to restructure them and align them strategically back to the values of Humana, with an enhanced focus on healthcare delivery.

Here was a chance to take a group of 39 disparate medical centers, all with individual working models, pull them together across multiple counties, and make them a functioning business unit. Ironically, the project was tailor-made for an entrepreneur.

I succeeded at this project and was quickly asked to take on more responsibility within the company. I was promoted and relocated twice with increasing responsibility and authority each time. Then came the opportunity to lead an organization with a strong legacy and brand, but one in need of growth and optimization.

The Wow Moments of owning my own companies had taught me to believe in myself and my team, to focus on hiring the right talent, and to ensure they were in the roles that allowed them to optimize their skills.

It also taught me to never lose sight of the customer experience. Nothing was more important.

I accepted the opportunity.

My goal was to establish a string of medical centers that no other hospitals or clinics could compete with because our patients would refuse to go anywhere else.

The company is called CAC Florida Medical Centers. The CAC stands for Clinica Asociacion Cubana. The first clinic was started in Cuba 50 years ago, thus the name, and then expanded into South Florida with the influx of Cuban Americans living in Miami. The working model for each center is special. I call it an all-in-one facility. A patient can see his or her primary care physician, specialist, dentist, or optometrist in one visit. He could see his ophthalmologist and get his prescriptions filled without ever leaving the building. It was a good experience. My goal was to make it a great experience.

The company's corporate offices were in Doral, so I knew the area well. And because a majority of our patients were Cuban, an added benefit was that I also spoke and understood Spanish.

From the beginning, I saw a special opportunity to implement the concepts of the WOW Moment, even if I hadn't defined it as such yet. Every business has customers and clients with expectations and a special set of needs, and the healthcare industry is no different. As with any industry, the difference lies in the services we provide. You see that every day in your own business, either as an owner or employee.

The challenge for all of us then becomes a matter of differentiating ourselves from the competition.

This was true with my first company, Network Connections Group, when we were recruiting talent for the IT world. If our recruits weren't a step above the rest, then there was no reason for IBM or Enterprise Rent-A-Car or MasterCard International to use us. It was true for Spectra Care when we were providing home healthcare. If we weren't providing an exceptional experience for our patients, then why would a physician recommend such a small company. And I could see that it was just as true for CAC. There were plenty of hospitals and clinics in South Florida, and my goal was to make us the standard bearer. I wanted to create a patient care model that everyone else wanted to emulate.

Even before my arrival, CAC had been a company long organized around service. They were already doing a good job in the communities they served.

My first task was to change what I saw as a cultural misconception within the company. Very shortly after I took the reins at CAC, I found that most of the people at the management level saw their role as one in service to our corporate offices in Doral, and their actions reflected this.

My first and most important job at the outset of my tenure was to change the tone and conversation within our own organization and with our individual associates on this very matter.

The message was simple and clear: Going forward, our corporate entity exists for one purpose and that is to serve our medical centers.

"The medical centers are where the magic happens," I told every one of my management team, and I expected that philosophy to be delivered company-wide.

For years, corporate had been the place to be. For years, corporate was the power. No longer. "From now on, we will recognize that the medical centers where our customers are serviced is where the power lies. Going forward, corporate exists to service the medical centers that are the heart and soul of our existence. And our actions are going to reflect this."

This was a 180-degree shift in the company's thinking. From now on, we would be focusing our on relationships with our patients and with one another. My learning journey, as I called it, had begun. And the learning journey of my leadership team and our associates company-wide had also just begun.

I wanted them to understand that the men and women at our medical centers were touching the patient every single day. What could be more important? What these men and women did every day was critical to our long-term success and our overall strategy as a company.

As for the people sitting in the C-level suites in our corporate offices in Doral, myself included, our organizational focus going forward would reflect this new attitude: we exist to serve our teams. These are the people touching our customers every day, the people selling, in essence, our product: the best healthcare in South Florida. Out with the old and in with the new.

From now on our task would be connecting on all levels. From now on we would be promoting relationships within the company and without. From now on, we would be raising the bar of our service basic to a place of superior experiences.

The concept of the WOW Moment was born.

As leaders, we all know that our job is to provide purpose, motivation, and direction to our team. All well and good. But the real challenge is getting everyone to truly buy in to what we are selling. It was easy for me to sit in front of them and say, "From now on, we at corporate exist to serve our medical centers. That's where the magic happens." I was the CEO. I didn't expect a negative response. I didn't expect anyone to stand up and say, "That's not the way it's going to be."

When the CEO at any company makes a strategic proclamation, especially the new kid on the block, people will most often say they are onboard even if their actions contradict their words. Resistance to change is natural, in particular when the change in strategic direction is as drastic as the one I was advocating.

In my case, saying it wasn't enough. I had to lead by example. And that meant stepping into the shoes of the very people who made the magic happen for CAC, the people at every level inside our medical centers. I spent a day as a referrals clerk. I answered the phones. I shadowed nurses and doctors. I talked to patients and pushed wheelchairs. I helped the janitorial staff.

At every staff meeting at every level, I designated one empty chair for the patient. We began every meeting the same way. I would say, "Everything we talk about, we talk about as if one of our patients is sitting in this chair. That way we're always focused on one question: how does it benefit the patient?"

By focusing on the patient, we began to change the way we were thinking. Now our efforts were directed at our medical centers; as I called them, the place where the magic happens. Now we were looking at how we could elevate the experience of the most important person in the company: the customer.

CHAPTER SIX

Defining Success (And Moving Beyond It)

The first question I always ask about any new process, procedure, or program is: how does it make the patient experience better?

If I sit down, hypothetically, with my senior leadership team and a proposal is made to streamline our referrals process, we start and finish with the patient experience. In your industry, you might call it the client experience or the customer experience, but it all translates into how each and every thing we do affects the end user. It doesn't begin with how this change might save us a half million dollars or a thousand hours a year. It doesn't begin with finances, accounting, or marketing. If my team can prove to me that a change in our referral process from a patient's primary care physician is in the patient's best interest, then we can talk about feasibility and process.

The equation is simple: without the patient, customer, or client, we're not in business anymore.

So if it disrupts what the patient expects and deserves or in some way disrupts service, it doesn't make sense. And if it doesn't produce a genuine WOW Moment somewhere down the road, then it doesn't make sense either.

Too many managers inside too many companies think first about the internals: time and money, procedures and policy. They think about their own convenience and how it affects them. This does not fit the WOW Moment concept that puts the customers first. If you're talking about *their* time, *their* money, and *their* convenience, then the equation makes sense.

Given our example, let's say someone proposes that all referrals from a patient's primary physician will henceforth be given to the physician's Medical Assistant rather than to the patient himself. The MA will immediately input the referral into the center's system and alert the scheduling department. Now, when the patient returns to the checkout counter or reception area, everything has been processed for him or her. Now, the patient no longer has to find the appropriate person to hand the referral to, and he or she no longer has to wait while it's processed. The patient is no longer acting as a conduit between members of our staff. The process is now seamless. Throw in the fact that transportation has already been arranged for those patients who don't drive, and the result is a far better experience for our customer. In fact, a good number of patients will see it as a WOW Moment. What's more, the decision-makers in corporate are now focused on the right thing: the customer experience.

———

The WOW Moment concept is not for everyone. I found early on that it requires hiring the right candidates, in particular because the idea most often requires a change in your company culture.

———

The company culture at CAC was considerably different than those at Spectra Care and Network Connections Group, where I was building a business more or less from inception. We had few employees, and I was in a position to really weed out candidates that didn't match the profile we were developing.

Now I've got a company at CAC that, at the time I came onboard, had nearly 700 employees. You can't fire everyone and start all over again; that was neither realistic nor necessary. There was a tremendous number of good people working at the company when I arrived.

I did, however, begin a process that I call "grafting." Grafting is a process of identifying, very early on, those people who understood the WOW Moment concept and could grasp what was involved in moving beyond the service basic of our centers to create exceptional experiences for our patients, and placing them in specific roles or departments.

Grafting is about finding people who see what they're doing in the workplace as more than a job; it's a calling.

No mistaking that such a search takes a ton of assessment and considerable work. One of the first steps we took when I arrived was to tweak our performance appraisal to include not only the hard skills necessary to meet the basic criterion of any particular position, but soft skills such as interconnectedness, interactive communications, and customer relations. I began to retrain my C-level team, our department heads, and our medical directors around this combination of hard and soft skills. In many cases, it was relatively dramatic. Here I was telling them, "These are the things we're looking for in our people going forward. So, from now on, these are the things that really matter to you."

If you're selling a change in culture to your people – especially if you're the new arrival – there is always a certain amount of resistance. I was okay with the resistance. I was okay with concerns and questions. But as the company's CEO, I had to improve our standing in the South Florida medical community. I had a clear vision of the company culture I wanted at CAC. It was my job to understand any resistance and turn it into a "buy in." Yes, the WOW Moment concept was the new guy's strategy, but I needed everyone to see why it would benefit us in good will as well as the bottom line, and get behind it with the same enthusiasm I had for the idea.

We'd been focusing primarily on process. We'd been focusing on the service basics. That's exactly what our competitors were doing.

If we didn't start moving from the basics to the experience and eventually to an extraordinary experience, somebody would surely get there before us.

Winning long term meant creating a mindset that focused on the creation of WOW Moments, the experience made extraordinary. That's how you create a brand that the customer naturally gravitates to. Ironically, once you get there, you don't have to spend as much on marketing and you don't have to spend as much on recruiting, because those patients and their families become the best marketing agents you could ever hire. When they're telling other people in the community, "You need to come experience the care at CAC. My doctor, their nurses and their staff, the entire center is awesome," you've created the best marketing vehicle there is. No print, TV, or radio advertising can compare.

As a leader, you always have to know the answer to the question: What defines success? Your team has to know how important this benchmark is as well or they are shooting in the dark.

I recall a major project that I managed for Humana while in Louisville. The company had twice missed its deadline in delivering a comprehensive set of marketing materials to its nationwide network in order to take full advantage of the selling season in late fall and winter. The biggest problem was a lack of enrollment applications for a sales staff who therefore found themselves behind the competitive curve.

My first step in solving the problem was to begin with the end user, the guys and girls in the field: the marketing consultants and the sales support staff. The product had to be designed for them, so why not design the process around their input.

Early on in the process I asked Jim Murray, our company's COO, how he defined success, and he replied, "Every piece of marketing and sales material has to be in everyone's hands by October 1." That meant 1,700 locations and 2,000 sales agents.

So that October 1 deadline represented success in his mind. "And what if we could get the material there before that?" I asked.

"Wow, that would be awesome," was his answer. What I had learned of Jim was that he was tough, but fair, and expected flawless execution of a plan. He was someone I admired and wanted to be like.

I realize looking back that delivering the marketing material ahead of schedule would be his WOW Moment. And that's what we did. The last of our 1,700 locations received their materials by September 26 and Humana had one of its greatest revenue years ever. We had defined success, and then went beyond that to the WOW.

It was shortly thereafter that I was offered the position at CAC. Inherent in the position was sufficient autonomy to satisfy my entrepreneurial spirit, and that has proved to be a good thing for all parties involved.

It doesn't matter what industry you're in, and it doesn't matter the size of your company, the WOW Moment concept is always based upon the end user.

If you and your company, big or small, service oriented or product oriented, are developing strategy and the tactics to carry out that strategy, focusing on your end users and their expectations and experiences provides a competitive edge like no other.

In my business, it's the patient. In the home construction business, it is the person who's eventually going to own the home. If you're in the hotel business, it is the patrons who are staying there for a night, a week, or a month. In any and all cases, your focus is always going to be the realization of their expectations, meeting those absolutely, and then having an understanding about what goes beyond those expectations.

Those are the steps necessary to get to the "Wow."

Service is not enough. Service is a basic expectation. To have lasting value and lasting relevance in the eyes of the customer, it is a matter first of creating an experience out of the expectation and then making something extraordinary of the experience. That is the WOW Moment, and the residue is just as powerful and long-lasting as the moment itself.

In moving from one industry to the next, I always remind myself that sales and service are essentially the same; both are foundational.

If your company sells a customer a product that he or she wants, you've met that expectation. You've satisfied the basic. But if you begin to understand more about how that customer plans to use the product, it has the potential of becoming more of an experience. If you can use the purchase of that product to learn more about your customer, suddenly you're adding value to the relationship overall. Once you've connected on this level, understanding what it takes to create a WOW Moment for that customer begins to crystallize.

Let's imagine that I am a salesman in an electronics store, for example, and a customer comes in looking for a digital tape recorder. I listen to her needs; she wants something that works well in a boardroom setting, something that can pick up a multitude of voices clearly in case the tapes need to be transcribed. That is how she defines success. I show her several products that do just that. Then I show her one that can easily download the audio onto her computer as an MP3 file, which can then be sent directly and in seconds to her transcriber. Her expectation is to record the board meeting clearly and concisely. Now, all of a sudden, she can have it in the hands of her transcriber within moments. She saves time and demonstrates her ingenuity.

She says, "Wow. Better than I imagined," and, just like that, I've created a WOW Moment. I took her basic expectation and created an experience just by understanding her needs – and her definition of success – and moving beyond them.

I can't name an industry in which this model does not work. I can't name an industry in which knowing what the end user wants, understanding his or her definition of success, and creating an extraordinary experience that transforms that definition doesn't benefit your long-term success and that of your company.

CHAPTER SEVEN

A WOW Moment Environment

When you're trying to identify an end user's needs, it all starts with a conversation.

All connections begin with some form of communication. When you're trying to identify a customer's expectations, whether it happens to be a visit to one of our medical centers or a trip to Best Buy for a piece of electronics, that conversation has to lead to a certain level of trust. Whether you're a salesperson at a retail store or a nurse at a healthcare facility, you can't create a trusting relationship if you look at your position solely as a paycheck. That suggests rather strongly that you just don't care enough to take the necessary steps to create a powerful line of communication.

If there is something beyond a paycheck that gets you up every morning, then the idea of developing relationships in the workplace makes sense to you.

If discovering a customer's needs and expectations makes sense to you, and if the idea of creating an exceptional experience beyond the service basic actually excites you, then you will begin to understand the concept of the WOW Moment and begin to envision how powerful those moments can be.

It is also safe to say that needs and expectations are not the sole purview of our clients or customers. We all have them. From the top of an organization to the bottom. At work and at play, in the home and in the community.

With a view on the workplace, I know that my associates have expectations that they want me to be aware of, and that they also want their immediate manager to be aware of. The fulfillment of those expectations reflects on their performance within the workplace, and they should be encouraged to spell out those needs and wants. I want to know what the members of my team expect to get out of their jobs, above and beyond a paycheck, and it's up to me to provide a work environment where the reality of those expectations can be met.

Your industry is no different. Without an enthusiastic workforce, it can be hard to sell the WOW Moment concepts. It's a two-way street. An employer has to ensure that his or her company is populated with the right kind of people. He or she also has to provide a positive work environment where these people are embraced, empowered, and can succeed.

An unenthusiastic salesperson at Best Buy is no different than an uninspired nurse in one of our medical centers.

Rather than making connections and forging relationships, you have people who are driving your clients to seek products and services elsewhere.

Customers, clients, or patients – whatever term you use to describe the end user in your industry – are not dumb. They can sense indifference in a worker just as easily as they can energy. They can sense a disconnect just as easily as they can engagement. They can sense a lack of loyalty just as easily as they can commitment.

WOW Moments are not just for our clients. You and I can provide them within our companies as well. For example, I have to focus on providing the occasional WOW Moment for my senior leadership team so they can get a taste of what it feels like. WOW

Moments are most effective when they are paid forward. There is a definite give and take even within the employee and employer relationship when it comes to the WOW Moment concept.

Our employees have expectations much the same as our customers: getting paid on time; coming to a safe work environment every day; being treated with respect; perhaps receiving certain benefits, such as medical insurance. How then do you go beyond these expectations to create an experience? For example, you add elements to the workplace that create a learning environment. You add an element of fun to the workplace. You allow a certain amount of autonomy. You encourage participation in the strategic planning process. These are just a few possibilities, but you understand my point. Imagine hearing someone say, "Oh, I wasn't expecting these kinds of opportunities or exposure. This is great."

Then you go a step further and celebrate their accomplishments in a public forum. You post the employee-of-the-month's photo in the lobby. You recognize birthdays. You take an interest in their kids. Imagine stopping by someone's work station and asking about the son's soccer game or the daughter's recital. Imagine hearing that someone say, "Wow, that was cool." Now you have an employee who understands what a WOW Moment can look like, and now they are much more able and willing to pay that forward with your customers and clients.

Promoting experiences within the organization has a ripple effect, and the goal is that the end user is the final recipient.

At CAC, we have a monthly newsletter dedicated exclusively to sharing letters that we have received from patients regarding the quality of their care. These kinds of letters tend to generate a lot of emotion because of our focus on healthcare, and a handwritten letter says so much more than an email or a voicemail. I want that impact to be enjoyed by everyone. I want the recipient of a patient's praise to have a platform where his or her behavior is celebrated because they created a WOW Moment. On the one hand, I want to honor that, but I also want that action to serve as an inspiration to others. As you might imagine, there is a ripple effect. By promoting behaviors that I see as appropriate for our employees, it actually prompts more people to look at the experiences these letters describe and want to create them themselves.

Employees most certainly look to their leaders for behavioral traits they can emulate. More than anything, they are looking for someone who cares about them.

There is the old saying that says: Employees don't care how much you know until you show them how much you care. Do you recognize their accomplishments? Do you connect with them? Do you truly demonstrate how much you care?

As the head of our company, I am asking my employees to make a viable connection with our patients – our customers, if you will – and to build relationships with them that create not only an experience, but an extraordinary experience. I could not ask less of myself. It is part of my job to lead by example, and incumbent in that is building relationships and making connections with my team, from top to bottom. Leadership is about knowing the people who work for you. It's about fundamentally trying to know who they are, as individuals, as people, as members of society. Knowing what makes them tick, not just as doctors, or nurses, or administrative help, but as men and women. My associates have the right to ask:

Do you care about me just the same as you do our patients and customers? If the answer isn't yes, then I have a problem.

The same dynamic applies across industries, in businesses big and small, whether you have one employee or a thousand. You have to figure out how to connect with the people you're asking to connect with your end user (customer).

―――

You have to understand your employees' expectations and their definitions of success, and you have to do everything you can to create a meaningful experience for them in the workplace.

―――

The dividends are unlimited, not the least of which is presenting them with the occasional WOW Moment. The ripple effect of that is their enthusiasm in delivering WOW Moments to your customers and clients, which is the bottom line to everything we're discussing here.

Our goal is always to deliver WOW Moments to our end users. When it comes to our products and services, this means our customers, our clients, our patients. But who is the end user for your HR department? Who is the end user for a department head or a supervisor? It is your employees. These are the people you're asking to take a customer experience and make it extraordinary. They deserve the same treatment from above. I expect my HR department to go above and beyond hiring and firing and processing compensation. I expect them to create WOW Moments for my associates. I expect the same from my department heads and my supervisors. What would those look like? Sure, a WOW Moment might be a substantial raise in pay. But very often it's simply a matter of recognition. It's about acknowledging their good work, saying thank you for putting in a great day, patting them on the back and saying, "I saw you with that customer. It was awesome. You really hit it out of the park."

C-Level managers cannot deliver WOW Moments locked in their offices. Managers cannot deliver WOW Moments if they're not walking the floors, lending a hand, and making contact.

A positive employee experience is just as important as a thriving customer experience, because the former makes it that much easier to enhance the latter. Happy, productive, self-motivated employees know what a WOW Moment feels like, which makes it that much easier for them to raise the experience of their customers to something extraordinary.

I can picture a department head sitting down with his sales group and saying, "You guys have all been doing a terrific job, and I appreciate it. I thought about the idea of a special gift for the top salesperson in the group, but I'm not going to do that. I want to give that to each one of you. I want each of you to pick out something you've been wanting and call it a thank you gift from me." He doesn't give them a gift card to any particular store. Instead he gives each of them a voucher for a hundred dollars with the caveat that they have to spend it on themselves. It's not extravagant, but it's personal. And when interaction with your employees is personal, it's also more meaningful.

When you're creating experiences – and here we are referring either to the customer experience or the employee experience - it takes work. It takes involvement. You truly have to care. Caring is time consuming. Too many people want the quick microwave popcorn approach. They don't want to take the time to pop the real deal. "No, it doesn't taste as good, but there's less hassle." It's easy to default into that kind of thinking.

As the leader of your organization, it's your job to set the tone for your organization, and that requires involvement, participation, and an indefatigable belief in the culture you're creating.

It is my job as the company CEO to set the tone for my direct reports, the men and women who represent the senior leaders in the company, and for every associate in our employ, right down to the janitors.

Certainly, my job is about developing strategy, stating our purpose, and communicating our direction, but if I don't connect with people up and down the company ladder, getting a "buy in" on my strategy, purpose, and direction is going to be difficult.

Shaping experience and getting to the "wow" begins at the top.

CHAPTER EIGHT

A WOW Moment "Buy In"

I was three weeks into my tenure as CEO of CAC when I showed up unannounced at one of our Miami medical centers. I went straight to our referrals department and said, "Good morning. I want you all to know that today I'm a referrals coordinator."

The response was a dubious, but curious, "Really? The company CEO is working with us today?"

After the shock had worn off, I explained that I wanted to experience a day in the life of a referrals coordinator, right down to the nitty-gritty details. I wanted to experience the bureaucracy, the frustration, and the challenges. I wanted to experience the fun and the camaraderie. I wanted to answer the phones. I wanted to follow up with patients. I wanted to take orders from the department head. The full package.

I made it clear this had nothing to do with looking over their shoulders. It wasn't a punishment. It was my way of understanding exactly what goes on once a referral is made. What about the system did the men and women in the department like. What didn't they like. What works. What doesn't.

It was a tremendous experience. While I was there, I was able to observe the referral process from start to finish. I was able to hear in person what part of the process needed fixing, and perhaps why certain things that needed fixing had gone unanswered. One woman told me that in 16 years on the job, not one C-Level executive had ever paid them a visit. That was her WOW Moment.

The next day I received a group email from the entire department thanking me for taking the time to experience their world, and that was a WOW Moment for me. It wasn't a token visit. Now I was able to respond to their needs, and now I would be able to introduce the WOW Moment concepts into their particular environment, firsthand.

———

I wasn't just a figurehead in the corporate office making policy.

I had created a connection.

I had planted the seeds of a relationship.

———

The experience also added an element of ownership on behalf of the men and women in that department for their part in the company. I had demonstrated my loyalty to them, and in return received an added level of commitment and enthusiasm from them.

The experience also proved to be an effective example to the rest of my management team. Now that we were committed as a corporate office to serve our medical centers, as opposed to them serving us, it became clear that such commitment meant a hands-on approach with the people at ground zero, at the place where the magic happens.

I didn't stop with the referrals department. I spent time in transportation and disease management departments. I sat at a desk with the people in our call center and nursing departments. I even set up tables and chairs at patient events coordinated by our marketing department.

This was not for show. It didn't matter that I was the CEO. I could have been the head of nursing or the head of our janitorial services. If you're in management, it's your job to know how things function or don't function at every level. Then, when you introduce a change in protocol or the institution of a new process, the men and women on your team know it's not coming from some lofty, insulated office somewhere, but from someone with understanding and perspective of what is required to be successful.

Leadership is, after all, a proactive proposition. You can't create an experience from the sidelines or sitting behind a desk. And you can't sell your team on a change in culture if you're not actively living that change. It doesn't work.

I wasn't shaking things up just for the sake of it. We not only had a goal of refocusing our energy away from the bastions of the corporate offices and onto our medical centers, I was also intent upon making the both the patient experience and the associate experience something exceptional. That would be impossible without a concrete feel for that experience.

WOW Moments are part of life as a whole, not just a workplace phenomenon. They infuse our personal lives as well. Giving your wife flowers might constitute an experience, but delivering them in person to her office would be extraordinary.

Calling your mom in the middle of the day might be expected, but dropping in unexpectedly to go to lunch takes it to the next level.

We've all seen our expectations exceeded. We've all had an experience that grew into something uncommon, something that makes us stop and say, "Wow. That was extraordinary." When you've experienced a WOW Moment, the knowledge makes it so much easier to create one for someone else: a family member, a friend, an associate, or the end user in your workplace.

Part of my job is to frame the concept for the 700 or so people in my employ. It goes back to human behavior. The example I like to reference is that we don't necessarily know joy until someone helps frame it for us. The WOW Moment concept is no different. The CEO showing up in the referral department of one of our centers and answering the phone right alongside the rest of the staff was a good example. It was unexpected. It was well received. And along the way I heard a few "Wows."

Once the WOW Moment concept has been experienced and is within grasp, it can be paid forward.

Let's step away from the healthcare industry again and look at a different kind of service culture, one developed by the Disney Corporation at their theme parks and on their cruise liners. While most companies are predicated on their ability to effectively service their customers or clients, that is not enough in this changing economic environment. As we've been saying, you have to create the experience on top of the service basics and the WOW Moment on top of the experience, making it extraordinary. Foundationally, Disney is clearly an example of a company that has mastered the service culture and taken pains to create an exceptional experience for the men, women, and kids who pass through the gates of Disneyland and Disney World every year.

The Disney model begins with the concept of defining excellence. The chain of excellence as their company sees it sounds rather straightforward, but it truly sets the tone for everything else.

It looks like this: **Leadership Excellent > Associate Excellence > Customer Satisfaction > Financial Gain/Repeat Business**

As you can tell, words are important in the service culture of Disney. Words set the tone for their actions. Customers are referred to as "members." That's how important the customer is in the scope of business relations at Disney. Everyone who visits their facilities is a part of the Disney family, and their satisfaction is second to none.

Done correctly, Disney's "members" directly affect the financial gain of the company and the immense repeat business they experience because these people then become the company's net promoters. They are out in the marketplace saying, "Oh, my goodness, I had such a great experience at Disney. We had the best time. And it wasn't just the rides. It was everything." In other words, it was the "experience." It was the people, it was the grounds, it was the attention to detail.

What we are defining here in this book as a WOW Moment, Disney defines as excellence. Much like in our model at CAC, the WOW Moment experience begins with leadership, extends to the entire Disney team, and becomes a reality with the customer (the member).

Here's a personal example. A close friend once took his family on a Disney cruise ship in the Caribbean, where the "member experience" is just as strong as it is at Disneyland or Disney World. One morning, the family just missed the buffet breakfast that regularly features all the Disney characters coming together in the dining hall, and his son was devastated. The disappointment must have shown on his face, because the maître d' pulled my friend aside: "Don't worry. I'll work something out."

And sure enough, he did. The next morning, there was a knock on the door of their stateroom, and lo and behold, there stood Minnie Mouse and Mickey Mouse delivering breakfast personally to his son. You can imagine his elation. You can also imagine how impressed my friend was that the maitre d' went out of his way to arrange such a special treat out of an apparent disaster.

Two years later, and the entire family is still talking about it. His son experienced a WOW Moment and so did the family.

Since then, they have recommended the Disney Cruise experience to who knows how many people, and he and his family returned a season later.

———

For me, my friend's story is a perfect example of a company culture founded in service and experience that ultimately begets a WOW Moment.

———

The last piece in the Disney Excellence model is the Financial Gain and Return Business that results from it.

Yes, financial gain and return business are part of the WOW Moment concept as well, and I want my employees to understand this. No, they don't need to know the fine details of CAC's profit and loss statement or balance sheet, but it is in their best interest – and mine – that they fundamentally understand that businesses are in business to make money, which, when all is said and done, allows them to employ people.

When a man or woman understands that his or her employment hinges upon the success of the company they work for, going beyond the service basics to create positive experiences for their customers is not only the right thing to do, but it also contributes to job security and adds to the bottom line.

Most importantly, this understanding also adds to a sense of ownership and responsibility. Now employees are no longer thinking outside the business; now they are thinking inclusively, as in, "I'm part of this. It belongs to me too."

At CAC, we use the term "La Familia," which means the family. This term encompasses every associate, from the top of the company to the bottom, and it includes our patients. We're all family. So when patients come to CAC for medical services, they can expect to be treated like family. We call our patients by name. We make a point of knowing something about their backgrounds. We make a point of knowing their kids too.

When it comes to patient care, we don't rush our physicians. We want them to explain things carefully and answer questions thoughtfully. If a patient says to one of our doctors, "Do you mind praying with me?" they stop and they pray, because that's what is needed at the time. We empower our associates to take whatever action is necessary to enhance La Familia, because it's this service component that links to the overall experience. Now, making the experience extraordinary comes naturally.

The WOW Moment concept is about personalizing the workplace, from the corporate office to the sales floor or the corridors of a medical center, and culminating in an experience that makes the customer or the patient feel like family.

The Disney model portrays it as a seamless chain beginning with leadership excellence and progressing naturally to associate excellence and finally to unrivalled member satisfaction. It works in corporate America. It works in medium-sized and small businesses. It works in one-person shops. It works in the community. It works at home. Create a WOW Moment, and the ripple effect has no bounds.

CHAPTER NINE

Success and the WOW Moment

Now let's talk success and how the WOW Moment concept can take success to new heights.

If we look at the Disney model, they define success as a balanced approach to quality. It looks like this: **Quality Employee Experience + Quality Customer Experience + Quality Business Practices = $uccess!**

Once the company has established an environment where its employees feel valued in their roles – a crucial point regardless of the industry and one we talked about in our previous chapter –

everything else revolves around a quality guest experience. Whether we're talking, in this example, about Disneyland, Disney World, the Disney Cruise Line, or any of the company's other entertainment enterprises, the company culture is guest driven, or, as they refer to their guests, "member" driven.

The people walking through the gates of their theme parks or boarding their cruise ships are the central focus of everything they do. Their number one priority is attempting every day to exceed guest expectations. This is why they're in business. You're greeted with enthusiasm when you arrive, you're serviced with enthusiasm at every point of contact, and you're presented with entertainment unmatched in the industry.

The correlation between the Disney model and the WOW Moment experience is one I often like to make because the comparison fits every business reliant upon an end user. At CAC we are "patient" driven, from the office of the CEO to the doctors and nurses at our medical centers, to our maintenance people to the men and women in billing, referrals, and rehabilitation. Patient driven!

The patient, and his or her experience, is our primary and most important focus.

Our goal is to understand our patients' expectations of service and care (our products in a nutshell) and to go above and beyond them, to take their experience and make it extraordinary. And like Disney, that focus on the end user is the whole reason we're in business.

If you sell produce to local grocery stores, provide insurance for homes and cars, or build spec homes in urban neighborhoods, you understand the quality customer experience because your success depends on it. It's what keeps you in business. And what drives your business to new heights is exceeding your customers' expectations. Because when they say, "Wow, that was unexpected," you have a customer for life. You make certain the lettuce you're delivering is the freshest on the market. You make sure you call your customers with the best insurance quotes available and follow up as if they were your only client. You build a home that impresses your buyers from the minute they pull up to the curb and hits every mark when they walk from room to room.

At CAC, we define success as delivering a superior patient experience from the moment he enters our facility to when he returns home.

This means creating an environment that our competitors can't match. From the superior care of our doctors to the friendliness of our front desk, to the cleanliness of our restrooms, that is the goal of each and every one of our medical centers. We do this by creating what I call an "exceptional patient experience." When that is your number one goal, the financial rewards and the health of your bottom line take care of themselves.

Just like the Disney model, it's impossible to miss. You start with a customer-centric company culture. You make absolutely certain that your employees feel wanted and needed and that they understand that a quality customer experience is their number one priority. Weave this together with exemplary business practices –

where accountability and responsibility are visible throughout the organization – and the result is a successful business.

Much like Disney, this customer-centric model at CAC begins with the ultimate basic: Point of Contact. This sounds simple, but the ramifications are huge.

Any time one of our patients encounters a person, place, or thing associated with our company in general or our medical centers in particular, the interaction has to reinforce a positive customer experience. A point of contact might be the receptionist at one of our centers or a billboard reminding patients of our services and locations. In our business, we create a map of every possible point of contact, from our appointment desk to our restrooms, from our shuttle buses to our referral departments, from our advertising to our training, from our nurses to our doctors.

We create on-stage areas and off-stage areas, just like they do at Disney World. When employees put on a Disney uniform and walk into the park, they are immediately on stage and everything they do has to meet the expectations that their members have for a quality customer experience. Courtesy and helpfulness are the rules of thumb at every point of contact. Going the extra mile to make sure that customers have the ultimate experience, from the rides and the food to the gardens and the rest areas, is rule number one. If there are members present (customers), a Disney employee is on stage. When break time comes, they have specific off-stage areas where they can gather to use their cell phones or eat a snack or take a nap. But when they're in uniform and in the park, they're on stage and every point of contact is vital.

The same holds true for our medical centers. We have areas that are both on stage and off stage for the staff. We don't make phone calls in examination rooms, labs, or waiting rooms. We're connecting with our patients and making it a point to meet every service basic, and we're looking for opportunities to make their experiences extraordinary.

At Starbucks, every barista is expected to be on task the minute he steps behind the counter. At Apple stores across the country, employees are not allowed to wear their Apple shirts when they are outside the store, because that shirt signals to their customers that they are there to service their needs the way only an Apple store and its products can.

At CAC, the minute I pull my car into the lot of our corporate headquarters I am on stage, and my actions must signal that, regardless of where I am or who I am talking to, emailing, or texting.

If there is ever a time during the day that I need to be off stage, I actually go back to my car and drive off the lot. If I'm upset, distracted, or otherwise off my game, I'll take a moment to go somewhere away from the office and out of reach of my team. When things are settled again, I get back in the car and go back to the office. On stage again.

Every leader has to be aware of 'point of contact,' and has to deliver the importance of this concept to his employees. Every individual in an organization has to have a picture of this dynamic in his mind. Every person is responsible for knowing when he is on stage and off stage, and what defines appropriate behavior in each. It's not acting. It's a matter of knowing your job and respecting it.

This leads to the subject of a company's culture.

———

Success in an organization is dictated by what I call "Corporate Culture by Design." We cannot get to an understanding of the WOW Moment concept without it.

———

The Corporate Culture by Design is based around a system of values and beliefs that any organization – CAC, Disney, Apple, Starbucks, or yours – establishes that drives action and behavior and influences relationships in a positive way.

You can have a culture by design or one that just happens.

You can have a culture that is well defined or one that is open to interpretation by anyone with an opinion.

You can have a culture that is clean and understandable to all or one that is vague and indistinct.

You can have a culture that is goal oriented or one that lacks purpose and direction.

If yours isn't defined by the former of each of these descriptions, then your company is likely listing in the water if not sinking.

A Corporate Culture by Design has to be part of your everyday work environment.

You can think of it in terms of the language that you use or the symbols that represent your company. At Disney, a customer is a *guest*, an employee is a *cast member*, and a ticket taker is a *park greeter*.

You have to establish a set of values that will be the hallmark of your company and share them openly and often with your team. At CAC, we order them as such: honesty, integrity, respect, courage, openness, and diversity. These are WOW Moment values. They are at the heart of our operation, and, when given the importance they deserve, they lead directly to WOW Moments within the customer experience.

As part of a Corporate Culture by Design, you recognize and reward your employees. You create a process that helps everyone get better. It looks like this: **Listen & Learn > Measure/Act/Remeasure > Recognize & Celebrate > Share > Listen & Learn.**

Now the road to success that we talked about earlier makes sense: Quality Employee Experience + Quality Customer Experience + Quality Business Practices = Success.

CHAPTER TEN

The WOW in Accountability

It is my job as CEO of our company and our medical centers to champion the WOW Moment concept across the organization, and I have a favorite story that demonstrates this far better than any pep talk I might give. So much so that we interviewed the patient in question, and the video is something I often show during my presentations.

The patient's name is Mrs. Rodriguez. She is 75 years old and came to us after a near-fatal car accident. In her words, she came into our medical center completely broken. "I couldn't walk, and I couldn't drive my own wheelchair. I was bandaged from head to foot," she told us.

One nurse, Diane Marrero, took a very special interest in Mrs. Rodriguez's recovery, and the day she returned to the center to begin her rehab, Diane was there to greet her. "She came right up to me, took my hand, and said, 'We're going to get you better.' And I could hear in her voice that she meant it. From that day forward, she was my angel. She truly became like a daughter to me. Every time I came to the center, Diane knew when my appointment was and she'd be right there waiting. She would wheel me right back to rehabilitation and motivate me every step of the way. And thanks to her, I'm walking once again. She's my angel."

This is a story packed with WOW Moments.

The very act of Diane meeting Mrs. Rodriguez that first day, taking her hand, and saying, "We're going to get you better," is a WOW Moment Mrs. Rodriguez will never forget. When Diane sat and watched the video and heard Mrs. Rodriguez calling her "my angel," she experienced her own WOW Moment. Listening to the story and seeing how these two women connected was a WOW Moment for me. Here was the new cultural shift I had introduced when I first arrived resonating throughout our organization, and it was a powerful realization for me.

So much is made these days of leadership accountability. And while there is considerable truth in this, we often forget that accountability is a two-way street.

The leader who suggests that his or her team will be held accountable for demonstrating this quality or satisfying that ideal, without being accountable for demonstrating those qualities and championing those ideals from the top down, is not a true leader.

Accountability begins at the top in every facet of our lives. If parents don't demonstrate responsible behavior and a willingness to bear the consequences of their actions, it's fairly certain that their kids will follow the same wayward path. If our government runs up astronomical debts, we shouldn't be surprised when such irresponsibility trickles down to the populace. If a CEO is not a practitioner of the culture he or she espouses, it will never take seed with the men and women in the trenches.

Accountability and a willingness to be responsible for our actions begin with structure. Human beings thrive on structure. We thrive on patterns. And as much as we fight the notion, our behaviors are positively reinforced around a system of structure and patterns. It begins when we're kids. As much as kids rebel, they like knowing what time to go to bed, what time to wake up, what time dinner will be served, how much free time they have, and how much time they have to spend doing homework. Parents demonstrate their accountability by setting this structure and building these patterns, and kids learn responsibility in maintaining these structures and patterns.

The same system of structure and patterns applies in the workplace. Part of a leader's job is to make certain that this structure and these patterns are in place and understood. At CAC, there is a structure and a formality in place around meetings and what's expected in those meetings. There is structure and formality in our processes and procedures, in our purpose and direction, in our duties, in our job descriptions, in our behaviors.

The better the structure and patterns surrounding these workplace parameters, the easier it is for people to understand what is expected of them.

Recognizing the expectations that have been placed on us makes us more accountable and more responsible. The byproduct is results. In the workplace, we are accountable for the results we produce and having definable structures in place makes these results more likely. A WOW Moment is a result that reaches beyond basic responsibilities, but it begins with knowing what those basics are.

It's not as difficult as it might seem. People like knowing what is expected of them. And what they like even better is exceeding those expectations. As leaders, we are charged with setting goals. We are charged with creating a strategy that moves our companies forward. Both the goals we set and the strategy that we develop are part of the structure and patterns we develop for our team. Inherent in these are the expectations we place on each team member. If you're in sales, it could be your numbers. If you're a nurse in a medical center, it could be quality patient care. If you're a teacher, it could be student performance.

As leaders, we are accountable for giving our employees the tools necessary to achieve these expectations. Our employees, on the other hand, are accountable for performing within the structure we've set for them, and they take great pride when someone in a leadership role says, "Wow, I didn't even think of that," or "Wow, you did that. Thank you. It matters."

―――

There is a perception that leadership and accountability

go hand-in-hand.

They don't.

―――

There are plenty of "leaders" in the workplace who actually fear accountability. They either set strategy and then turn a blind eye to the tactics necessary to implement it – a "see no evil, hear no evil" mentality – or they micromanage every move their team makes, a quick and easy way of stifling innovation and creativity.

Everyone has his own personal style. I have never seen myself as a CEO who needs to define every step his team members make, i.e. Step A, Step B, Step C, Step D, Step E. I set strategy. I make clear what our goals are. I am very clear with my team about the tactics and what success looks like to me. In fact I tell them: If you can jump from Step A to Step E directly, that's fine, just so long as you get there and the results meet expectations.

We've all seen examples of leaders who are afraid to set structure, give direction, and be accountable for the results, asking instead that people down the chain of command do so. That's not accountability. We've also seen plenty of managers who lord over every step in the process. They see micromanaging as accountability in the extreme, when, in fact, it demonstrates a lack of faith both in their own ability and that of their team. I always come back to the customers (our patients), and their overall experience. And while I can paint a picture of what a successful experience looks like, I don't try to define what the "WOW" will look like.

WOW Moments are relative to each situation and each patient (or customer). They are relative to what each patient expects and what each employee defines as an extraordinary experience.

I want to set the overall tone of the WOW Moment culture in our company, but it is personalized by each patient experience and how each employee perceives it. Ironically, this allows each employee to be accountable without someone looking over his or her shoulder every minute.

In every case, the customer, client, or end user defines the "WOW." It is up to the nurse or doctor or orderly who best knows the individual to identify it. And it's not hard. Once an employee understands the WOW Moment concept, it comes naturally. Sometimes a simple, well-meaning greeting is enough to provide one patient a WOW Moment, while it might take a shoulder massage or a piece of chocolate to get a "WOW" out of another one. One is not better than another.

The customers define the WOW Moment. The customers also tell you when you've hit the mark. They may say, "Wow! How nice." They may say, "Get out of here. I never thought of that." Or they might just smile the kind of smile that says, "Thank you for thinking of me."

We had an 89-year-old patient in one of our medical centers recently. She has a son in his late sixties. He has a developmental disorder that makes it difficult for him to take care of himself. His mother has been his primary caregiver for his entire life, cooking for him, cleaning for him, and essentially tending to his every need.

When the mother was hospitalized, and would be for at least a week, her biggest concern was not for herself but for her son. How would he cope? Who would cook his meals? Who would make sure he took his prescribed medicines? As it turned out, the nurses, medical assistants, and other staff familiar with her situation had no intention of letting this be a problem. They all got together, prepared meals on their own time, and delivered them to the son every morning. They made certain he was comfortable and taking his prescribed medicines.

For the son, the WOW Moment was the realization that these people cared enough about his well-being to go out of their way. For the mother, the WOW Moment was the realization that the nurses, medical assistants, and staff at the center had really been paying attention to her conversations. "It's not that I ever told anyone that I was the one providing his meals and making sure he was okay. The people at the center just picked up on it. They actually cared enough to pay attention."

That's a story I'm very proud to share.

Yes, this kind of extraordinary interaction is good for business, though that had little to do with the actions of my staff. In fact, this was uncompensated volunteer time. Interestingly, however, the real beauty of going beyond the expected and creating an exceptional experience is the feeling of satisfaction that it provides the person doing it. You take positive action, and the power of it comes back to you. You might call it a WOW Moment in reverse.

Accountability has a ripple effect. It's contagious.

We never know who's observing our actions. We never know who's listening. We never know whom we're influencing.

Who doesn't like it when they perform well? Who doesn't like it when they've been praised for their actions? While being responsible has consequences, I believe most people prefer the consequences of being responsible and accountable as opposed to the consequences of doing nothing, avoiding participation, and backing away from leadership. Contributing in a positive way feels good. Being reliable feels good. Setting a good example feels good. And people respond when they see someone contributing, being reliable, and setting a good example.

Accountability can be scary. It puts you on the spot. Now all of a sudden you're responsible to others and to yourself. Now all of a sudden people are relying on you. Now all of a sudden people are looking up to you. But that's what makes accountability rewarding. And that's a WOW Moment in its own right.

CHAPTER ELEVEN

Innovation and the WOW Moment

I always believe that we can get better, no matter what the endeavor. As a person, as an organization, in the workplace, or at home, we can always do better. We can always improve and grow. I think that is a healthy attitude, and it is the kind of attitude that inspires WOW Moments.

Getting better begins with recognizing achievement, and we should always applaud that. We should always take the time to celebrate improvement and advancement. But I don't think we're meant to stop there. As a business leader, I'm always eyeing the next thing. I'm always anticipating the next step.

And as my son will tell you, this outlook on getting better doesn't stop when I walk in the door at night. If he comes home with an A in science, that is an achievement to be immensely proud of and one that speaks highly of him. And we always take the time to acknowledge and celebrate his accomplishment. But we also take the time to explore how he can continue to get more out of his class.

I want him to feel proud of his approach to school, but I also don't want him to be completely satisfied.

We must stay hungry and curious.

I believe the very same for our company. I want us to proud of our forward movement. I want us to acknowledge and celebrate goals met. But I also want us to focus on taking what we've done well to the next level. Good can be great. I'm always thinking: How do we turn the dial up just a little? I want my team to be proud of every positive gain. I want them to recognize every positive step. Basking in accomplishment is a good thing. I also want them thinking about the next step. I always want them thinking about where we can go from here.

Evolution, whether it is personal or professional, has to be constant. Stagnation is a man's worst enemy. It is also a company's worst enemy.

We evolve constantly, and the more aware we are of our evolution, the more directed and enjoyable it can be. Innovation springs from that evolution. It is a product of a simple question: How do we get better? It is a product of constantly asking: What is the next step?

The philosophy is not a matter of size when it comes to the workplace. I went from leading a small company at Spectra Care with 200 employees to joining a Fortune 100 company with over 50,000 associates at Humana. Today I lead an organization with just under 2,000 associates. The premise is the same. You have to explore new ideas. You have to embrace innovation. You have to commit to the constant evolution of both the individual and the whole.

Some people say we are in a constant war against complacency. I don't believe that. I believe people are driven to improve and are driven to share new ideas. I believe that the men and women who make a difference in our world are rarely satisfied. They share the notion that they can always get better, that growth and change are the only constants. Innovation excites them.

They see the growing plague of entitlement as society's worst enemy, and they're right. Entitlement and innovation don't mix. Entitlement and the WOW Moment concept aren't a mix either. You cannot provide someone with a WOW Moment if all you're thinking about is how entitled you are to your own WOW Moment.

It is unfortunate in many ways, but we have become an entitled nation. We envy the man or woman who wins the lottery. We allow ourselves to be enticed by get-rich-quick schemes. We distill things into 30-second sound bites and come to think that even the good things in life come fast and easy. The truth, however, is so much different from that.

Before Steve Jobs' unfortunate passing, we often saw him plugging his Apple products on television or on the Internet, and we forgot that he worked for years making them a reality. He failed far more times than he succeeded. Ironically, we only see the IPhone or the Ipad and not the amazing innovation that was required to produce them.

We see Bill Gates and forget that his journey to the head of Microsoft began when he was a teenager.

We see our favorite movie stars and think they became famous overnight. We don't hear about the struggles and the rejection.

Edison built a thousand failed light bulbs before he hit on the right formula, but we don't appreciate the journey. We just want the light to work the moment we hit the switch.

We want it quick and easy. Our kids want it quick and easy. We want the microwave popcorn. We want the reward without the labor. That, however, is not where innovation comes from.

One of the things I say to my associates – and a number of them are exceptionally brilliant – is this: "You have to do your time in the mine. You have to get in there with a shovel and dig out the gold nuggets."

In other words, knowledge doesn't come easy. Innovation doesn't happen when you're sleeping. It takes work. And it takes a willingness to run head-on into a lifetime of obstacles.

These "learnings," if you will, are critical to a person's growth. They are essential to whatever success you hope to achieve down the road. I tell my son the same thing. Yes, I could make the road easier with a certain amount of financial assistance, but that doesn't truly help in the long run. It won't help him define the kind of man he wants to be, and it won't help him build something sustainable.

You have to go into the mine and do the heavy lifting. Innovation is work. The same is true when it comes to creating WOW Moments; whether it's a WOW Moment meant for people in the workplace, at home, or out in the community, it takes effort and thought.

———

You have to want to be innovative; it has to excite you. And you have to want to create WOW Moments for people; it has to come from inside you.

———

Interestingly, both innovation and the WOW Moment concept require a strong foundation. Companies that we define as innovative – like the Apples and the Microsofts of the world – have a sustainable quality to them that begins with a service culture and is built upon a definable understanding of the basics. We mentioned Steve Jobs and Bill Gates earlier. They didn't develop products and force-feed them to their customers. They understood what their customers wanted, and they developed products to fill that need.

———

Success is all about the end user and his or her needs. That is the makings of a sustainable model, because your innovation is then grounded in meeting those needs.

———

Innovation doesn't come out of left field. You have to be connected. You have to have your boots on the ground. You have to understand the end user.

WOW Moments don't come out of left field either. You have to understand the needs of your end user. Then you can be innovative in developing WOW Moments that truly resonate with each recipient.

You can't create WOW Moments sitting in your office with the door closed. You have to know what's going on with your people, and together you have to know what's going on with the end user.

Those gold nuggets we talked about don't come to you unless you grab a shovel and dig your way into the mine. You have to be eager for the discovery and undaunted by the prospect of failure. What most people don't realize until they've done this is that the discovery of those gold nuggets represents WOW Moments in their own right.

Back when I was running Spectra Care, our home healthcare business, we were thinking about expanding outside of our service model. One day we paid a visit on a potential acquisition. While we were out in the lobby waiting for our appointment, one of the center's patients came in, and I said, "Hello. How are you doing?"

In response, she said, "I really wish I could get this care at home. This is so exhausting."

The light when on. We'd discovered a gold nugget the size of a basketball.

We decided right then and there not to acquire a dialysis center at all, but to start our own home dialysis service. It was a decision that took our company to the next level, and all because we were out making connections, digging in the mine, if you will.

Now that we had the idea, we started asking questions. We began digging deeper. Was it possible, for instance, to take the very large dialysis machines which centers were using and convert them to more portable replacements? We talked to the manufacturers. We experimented with dollies and rolling platforms. We tried putting tires on the machines themselves. We stood them up. We laid them down. Finally, we found the machine we wanted. It was manufactured by a company called Baxter. But it didn't have wheels. We would have to install them ourselves.

We decided against tires in favor of softer rubber wheels. We found a welder who could effectively weld the wheels to the bottom of the machine, and we were in business. Not only were we in business, we were ahead of our time. That was a WOW Moment. It was a product of being out there, asking how and why over and over again, and listening to the answers. And then, like all WOW Moments, it was a matter of taking what we had learned and putting it into action.

Sometimes innovation is a light-bulb-moment. But generally, it's a product of taking an idea and working with it.

Dead ends are part of innovation. Asking endless questions is part of innovation. Listening and staying engaged are part of innovation.

Sometimes creating a WOW Moment for a customer is a matter of spontaneity. It just hits you, and you act. In our business, you see a patient and just know he or she is lost and in need of directions, or would like a private room with a view of the medical center's garden. But most times, you get to know a patient or a customer. You ask them the right questions. You listen to their answers, which opens a window on their needs. Then you see the possibilities of moving beyond those needs to something special. That discovery is special to you because you know how special it will be to your end user. A bona fide WOW Moment. You created an emotional attachment and you now have a customer for life.

I'll never forget a monumental moment in my development as a healthcare provider. I was talking with a friend of mine from undergraduate school. Her name is Ritsuko. Ritsuko is Japanese. I remember as clearly as if it were yesterday her observation that we here in America don't honor our elders like they do in Japan. Seniors there are revered for their experience and the knowledge they impart. In Japan, younger people seek out this knowledge, and they build upon it. In Japan they think long term, while here in America, she observed, everything is right here, right now.

That, I realized, is a fundamental problem because innovation has long-term consequences; it doesn't happen overnight.

———

WOW Moments are much the same, because their essence is based upon relationships and connections, which take time.

———

WOW Moments build loyalty, because they are so meaningful to the recipient. They spawn partners who will gladly sing the praises of your company and refer business. Most importantly, however, they also show respect for people deserving of it, and that's a lesson we should never forget.

CHAPTER TWELVE

Communication and the WOW Moment

When we talk about creating a corporate culture that supports the WOW Moment concept, the premise can be stated in a simple and concise phrase: we are here to serve. Simple and concise it might be, but there are multiple layers to this premise. The first and most important layer is that we as a company are here to serve the end user. The second and less often stated layer is that management is meant to serve the rank and file, in other words, those who develop product, service product, and sell product. This simple and concise message runs across all industries, whether you're selling cars, teaching yoga, or installing solar panels. If your bottom line approach to doing business is about serving the end user, then the corporate culture you're creating will look like this: Focus on **Service Basics** + Take Care of **Customer Expectations** (focused on creating an experience) = the creation of **Wow Moments**!

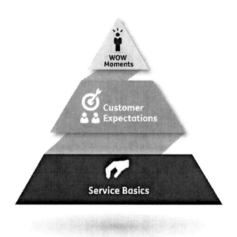

As a CEO, I like to turn the phrase "We are here to serve" into a more personalized, "I am here to serve."

The idea behind this obvious replacement of one pronoun with another is extremely significant. It conveys the message that a corporate culture of service has to begin at the top. If it doesn't, if the person at the top – man or woman – is only talking the talk and trying to convince everyone else of a strategy he or she doesn't truly live by, then it's just a sales job. You've shaped a culture of passing the buck and deception.

Creating WOW Moments is engrained in a philosophy I call "Servant Leadership." Servant Leadership took shape the day I pulled all of our associates at CAC together in a hotel for our first associate engagement get-together. I stood up before them and said, "I see myself as serving every single one of you. That's my role. And I see everyone on my leadership team as serving every single one of you too."

That was the day I knew I had effectively defined the essence of my job. That was the day I fully understood my role: to get all of the roadblocks out of my team's way so that they can press on with the business of serving our patients.

There was my role defined by three words: "I serve you."

There is a trickle-down effect to this attitude that solidifies the foundation of service that we've been talking about throughout this book. People get excited about coming to work because they know that management has their backs, and they know that they've been given a mandate to do their jobs without interference.

Now you have a place where people want to work.

Leadership under these circumstances is not a top-down proposition. Leadership is about lifting your team up from the below, supporting them, and recognizing that the success of your company is on their shoulders.

When a leader – any leader in any industry – clearly communicates to his or her team that, " I'm here for you. You're not here for me," that is the essence of truly great leadership. You've taken ego out of it. You've stood before your team and given them a bona fide WOW Moment that will resonate long after the moment has passed.

If, as a leader, you find yourself needing to get credit for everything of a positive nature that happens within your company, you're headed down the wrong path. It's not about being praised or seen or glorified. It's about doing the right thing when no one is looking and when there may be no applause.

Creating WOW Moments has a certain baseline. They should be fun, rewarding, and meaningful.

In our business, it begins with the idea of connecting with our patients and with their families, and making their experiences in our centers something positive and memorable.

I want every person throughout the company to know that a WOW Moment is a difference-maker. From a business perspective, I want them all to understand that the amount of patient loyalty that a WOW Moment generates is extraordinary. From a personal perspective, I want them to recognize how a WOW Moment can take the ordinary patient experience and create a unique "care" experience, one that we believe is nearly impossible for our competitors to replicate.

In our world – just as it is in the vast majority of industries – patients, customers, and clients have any number of choices. In our world, that includes the primary care physician they choose and the medical center they patronize. Is a WOW Moment experience enough to keep them coming to our medical centers and making us their first choice in healthcare? I believe it is. Customers in any industry want to feel special, and true WOW Moment experiences do just that.

I often remind my team that our medical centers are more than just places where our patients visit with their primary care physician, or where they see their friends in our wellness center for fitness activities. It's more than attending health seminars or receiving their prescriptions. I want our medical centers to be a place where our patients find inspiration. I want them to be a place where our patients can rely on our promise to take care of their health no matter what the circumstances.

The Service Experience we provide has a simple aim: to take our service from good enough, to great, and finally to "WOW."

The Service Experience is about creating emotional moments for our patients. And make no mistake, "Wow!" is an emotional response.

When patients feel welcomed and comfortable, and when they feel cared for and appreciated, the response is emotional. This is a blanket statement that you can make about almost any industry. And when your actions have generated an emotional response, you know you've made a difference.

A service experience can be as simple as looking up from whatever we happen to be doing at any moment and sharing a warm "hello" with a patient when she enters one of our medical centers. It can be as meaningful as stopping to talk with a family member waiting in the lobby and asking how everyone is doing. It can be as thoughtful as bringing coffee into the waiting room for a patient, family member, or friend.

For me and my team, one of the best WOW Moments we can experience is when a patient tells a friend how friendly everyone is at one of our medical centers. That conveys the reality of the emotional feeling you've created with her.

In your business, it might be receiving a referral from one of your customers. It might be receiving a bouquet of flowers or a small gift with a card that says: "Thank you." It might be a new order at double the size.

When you put a WOW Moment out into the world, it almost always comes back to you.

The WOW Moment concept doesn't always come naturally. Sometimes you have to play with the idea. I take it a step further by having our associates practice coming up with potential WOW Moment suggestions. I give them a pen and paper and say, "Improvise three WOW Moment ideas using the people you most often come in contact with. Think of their responses. If your idea elicits a 'Wow, that was unexpected,' then you've hit on something. Take an everyday experience with a patient and make it extraordinary."

Service experiences and making them extraordinary are about going the extra mile for your client, customer, or patient. Amazing things can happen when you're sincerely warm, friendly, and helpful. When you show people you truly care, whether at home, in the workplace, or out in the community, you tap into a universal need for connection and relationship. Now you've entered the realm of the WOW Moment.

A significant part of creating a new and dynamic corporate culture is the principles that govern communication within your organization. Make no mistake, there must be order and understanding about the way you communicate, what you'll communicate, when you'll communicate it, and how you'll communicate it. There has to be cohesion around your message and your mission.

Your company goals have to be well defined and shared across the board. No one on your team can have any doubt about what your company stands for. The message has to come from the top; this is a given. But how that message is conveyed is extremely important. The more direct, the better. The more personal, the better. The more inclusive, the more it will resonate.

With the WOW Moment concept, the aim is to create a culture destined to move beyond just basic service to the creation of an overall experience. Those can't just be words.

It is my job to determine how best to demonstrate what the service experiences should be. Here's where the governing principles of your communication vehicle come into play. Can I best convey this message, for example, via a written document disseminated to everyone in my organization? Would it be more effective to create a video or to combine a conference call with a Power Point presentation? Do I pull everyone together under one roof and communicate to them from a podium?

We talked earlier about the importance of structure and patterns, and this applies to your communication principles as well.

Communication must be consistent. It has to be honest and genuine, the good news with the bad.

CHAPTER THIRTEEN

Vision, Values, and WOW Moment Characteristics

Creating experience starts with an understanding of the service experience and the service basics specific to your industry and your business. Cars are not insurance. Building houses is different than printing newspapers.

We have to get the basics established from the top of the organization to the bottom and make sure that they're getting done correctly. And not just correctly, but with a sense of pride.

We begin by understanding the expectations of those we're giving service to or producing product for, and then we establish a process of delivering unexpected value and quality that exceeds these expectations. In this case it doesn't matter if you're building homes or printing newspapers; every person on the receiving end of your service basic has expectations. Understanding those expectations gives you the tools to exceed them. Don't just produce a good newspaper with an adequate sports section; give your readers the best reporters and make sure the paper lands on your subscriber's porch every morning.

In the healthcare industry, a big part of our job is providing guidance to our patients on any number of complex issues and building the kind of emotional engagement with them that shows how much we care.

Caring is the fertile ground of WOW Moments.

First of all, our patients often feel at the mercy of their medical condition. If our medical center's staff can educate and empower them to manage their condition, then they've already exceeded customer expectations.

One of our calling cards is: *We're in this together.* You can imagine how powerful such a message is in the medical world when it's sincerely delivered. But the truth is, it's a message that resonates in any industry. When you walk into an Apple store in the mall, the people wearing the blue Apple shirt want you to feel like you're a part of a club. You're special. You're what makes Apple special. We're in this together.

At CAC, we are very specific about the personal characteristics that we want our team members to exhibit. Being accurate is a high priority in the healthcare world. When people are "on stage" in our centers, they are expected to be correct, complete, thorough, precise, and error-free. This is about knowing your business inside and out. Being able to talk the talk and walk the walk. This is about being prepared. There are absolutes in the medical world, but there are few industries in which being anything less than accurate is acceptable, yours included.

From the top of our organization to the bottom, we must be reliable. It's a service basic.

In the workplace, this suggests a level of trustworthiness that is indisputable. It also suggests dependable service relationships and transactions in which confidence and confidentiality are never in dispute. It suggests a working relationship whose commitments and results are consistent, predictable, and controllable.

Our processes have to be easy to use, especially when it comes to our patients. We want to keep it simple and we want to make our interactions with our patients hassle-free, straightforward, and efficient. These are patient expectations. If you deal with end users at any level, keeping things clear and transparent is a must. At CAC, we make certain that any information a patient needs is available and that there is someone there to explain it if there is any misunderstanding. To do otherwise is unacceptable.

Being courteous goes without saying, but it is important to state it in any case. Interestingly enough, a show of courtesy is often taken as a WOW Moment in this day and age. At CAC, it's a given. We demand that our people be friendly and empathetic.

Empathy is a WOW Moment waiting to happen.

And an individual who is respectful and is willing to go above and beyond is not only part of our hiring process, but also acts as a tool that impacts every level of the service experience.

A huge piece of the WOW Moment concept is the need to be proactive. Taking an experience and making it extraordinary requires individuals knowledgeable enough about the person they are serving, or the situation they are attending to, to anticipate an end user's needs. Being proactive means reaching out when it's appropriate, lending a hand, and being willing to lead.

Last but hardly least among the characteristics we espouse in our company is the ability to personalize relationships whenever possible. This means looking at every customer as an individual with specific needs and making our responses relevant to those needs. When a physician is with a patient, we want that patient to feel as if he or she is her only focus. Talk about feeling special. Talk about the opportunity for a WOW Moment. If that physician is able to tailor a situation to fit the patient's need and personalize her responses, she'll hear a "WOW" response pretty much every time.

———

We can't build long-term relationships without a personalized connection. When customers feel valued, they respond with loyalty and commitment. Success is bound to follow.

———

With that in mind, I want my entire team to have a clear vision about what the WOW Moment concept can mean to our company, to each of them as employees, to each of them as people, as members of a community, as a spouse, a parent, a friend, or a family member.

When the men and women in your employ can see the value in their efforts and can see the short and long-term effects of creating WOW Moments, then you know you're building a strong, viable team.

If you're a house painter, and your customer comes home and sees the extra effort you've put into the trim around his house and how you have taken the time to replace the roof flashing, you'll know you've exceeded his expectations. You'll likely hear a "Wow, I really appreciate you doing that." And you'll create a customer advocate who will be singing your praises to all his neighbors.

You may have heard the saying: "Engaged stakeholders are more than loyal; they are priceless."

I like to add this as well: "And when engaged stakeholders are beyond satisfied, they are emotionally connected."

That is the makings of a powerful WOW Moment, and it goes for any relationship. WOW your wife with flowers the day before Valentine's Day and dinner out the night of, and you've taken the experience and given it a touch of the extraordinary.

You've heard the numbers. It costs six times more to attract a new customer than to retain an existing one. Plus, you're already connected to your old customers. You've got a relationship. And success is all about relationships.

People are always arguing about cutting costs. Sure, it's smart to know where your money is going and what it's creating and producing. But if you can increase your customer retention just 2% using WOW Moment concepts, it can have the same effect on your profits as cutting costs by 10%. The former strengthens relationships; the latter damages them.

———

The most important of all statistics is a little-known one that says that 70% of a customer's buying decisions are based upon positive human interaction.

———

This seems so obvious on the surface, but it is amazing how often we neglect this "human" need. Imagine the effect of a WOW Moment. All of a sudden you have an interaction that goes from positive to exceptional, and a customer's buying decision is an absolute no-brainer. You're their guy (or girl). Why would they buy from anyone else?

There is no way of making light of customer loyalty. I like to talk about the three layers of customer loyalty, and two of them are bad.

The first, and worst, is the Assassin. This is the customer whose experience with you and your company has been so negative that he goes out of his way to ruin your reputation and that of your company.

The customer who is Apathetic is nearly as bad. He's been driven by some action or lack of action to a point of not really caring. Getting him back is tough if not impossible.

And then there is the Advocate. The advocate doesn't just happen. In most cases, a customer has choices. In our business, there are any number of healthcare choices in Florida: hospitals, clinics, full service medical centers. If we want patients to choose CAC's centers and to choose them every time, we have to create an environment that our competitors can't match.

What does it suggest when two out of three of these customer mindsets are negative? It suggests that positive, strong customer relationships take work. That creating WOW Moments doesn't just happen. You have to know your customers and you have to truly care about them.

It takes vision. It takes a core set of values. It takes WOW Moment characteristics.

If you fail at the basics, if you let your customer down before you even get started, you're doomed. If you treat a customer poorly, rudely, or indifferently, plan on having an Assassin out there just waiting to pull the trigger on your business.

If you get the basics done right, if you demonstrate a certain accuracy in your work and a certain dedication to being thorough in your customer service, chances are good that customers will find you acceptable. There may be a certain apathy involved that may cause them to seek out your competitors, not because you've done a bad job, but only because they're not head over heels for you, your product, or your process. They certainly didn't experience a WOW Moment.

So then what is it that makes a difference, that turns an apathetic client into an advocate for you and your business? What is it that turns his experience into something extraordinary?

It begins with a proactive approach that demonstrates an outside-in focus, allowing you to get to know your customers so well that you can anticipate their needs and consciously go beyond them.

It begins when your relationship is personalized to the point where you are able to create an emotional engagement with your customers that solidifies their loyalty and turns them into advocates for you, your business, and your team.

It begins when you approach every day with a set of values that includes honor and integrity, values that include creativity and productivity that are forward thinking and honest, values that respect completely the relationships you've built with your clients.

Then the WOW Moments come naturally.

CHAPTER FOURTEEN

WOW Moment Outcomes

We have spent a good deal of this book talking about the fact that everything in business begins and ends with the end user. The customer, the client, or, in our case at CAC, the patient. This is the fabric that transcends all else in business simply because your business and mine depend on sales. Yes, even a medical center has to think in terms of sales. You can have the greatest product in the world – the best widget, the latest smartphone, a world class medical staff – but only when the end user puts down his or her hard cash to purchase what you're offering do we have something viable.

Now let's step backward in the process, looking from the end user back to the beginning, and study all the touch points that make for a successful customer experience. In our business, the first step back takes us to our associates. These are the people who man our medical centers, who identify the needs of the patients and recognize their expectations and then endeavor to exceed them, creating, in the best of circumstances, an extraordinary experience.

This is what I call a WOW Moment Outcome.

If we take a step further back in the organization, we come to the various levels of leadership: department heads, floor supervisors, C-level management, the office of the President and CEO. The long-term goal of leadership is to serve the factory floor, the sales forces, the medical staff, the teacher, the carpenter, the receptionist. The purpose of leadership is to build an army of people and equip them in the best possible fashion to serve the end user. That is the investment leadership has to make. That is my focus as the CEO in charge of 58 medical centers and nearly 2,000 people. The end result that every one of us has to be seeking – from my office in corporate to the nurses and doctors who are hands-on with our patients, to the receptionist in the lobby to bus drivers who ferry patients back and forth from their homes – is an exceptional patient experience.

In my service model, an exceptional patient experience translates into one thing: If a patient is in need of medical care, he or she thinks first and foremost of CAC.

I want an automatic response that says: "I'm going to my local CAC facility because I know they have my best interest at heart and will provide me exemplary care. I'm going there because I know I will leave feeling better. I'm going there because I won't feel like a number; I'll feel like the most special patient in the world. I'm going there because I know I'll leave thinking, 'Wow, that was special.'"

I want patients to come back every time they have a health concern because they've had a great overall healthcare experience in the past, because we've resolved any and all health issues they may have experienced and have demonstrated genuine concern and care.

There is really no difference between my business and yours. The industry in question doesn't matter. We're all striving for a WOW Moment outcome that ensures the loyalty and advocacy of our customers and clients. The teacher wants a child to leave her classroom with a smile on her face and sense of learning. A stockbroker wants his client to leave his office feeling as if he or she is the most important client he has, regardless of the size of their portfolio. The online bookseller wants his or her end users to receive a book so quickly and in such pristine condition that they say, "Wow, I'll never buy a book from anyone else."

Customers always have choices. Those choices are based upon the quality of the experience, but they are also based upon fiscal responsibility.

In your business and in mine, we have to make the financial aspects of any transaction work for all parties concerned. In the CAC model we are, essentially, paid to keep our patients healthy. Because we work with certain government programs, we are paid a fixed amount per patient. If a patient isn't feeling well, it is not only in his best interest to get him well quickly and keep him well, it is in the best interest of our business model as well.

If you take your car into the garage with a transmission problem, it is in the garage's best interest to do the job right for two basic reasons: one, you leave happy; two, you'll come back next time you have a problem because your expectations have been met. And if that garage owner also goes an extra mile by fixing a leak in your radiator pro bono, you're going to say, "Wow, I didn't expect that." And now he has a customer for life. It benefits no one if you have to take your car back because the garage did a shoddy job. You've wasted your time, and they've lost money in the process. Moreover, you'll never be back. Why would you? You have too many garages to choose from.

At CAC, our mandate is to fix the problem the first time, and to do it by creating a great patient experience. This demonstrates value for the patient and makes sense fiscally. It also makes sense based upon everything we've discussed about the WOW Moment concept. WOW Moment outcomes are never just about dollars and cents. They are about branding the customer with a mark of excellence. When that happens, you and your team feel a sense of accomplishment and satisfaction. Your customer is blown away by the service and product he's just experienced. You've made both a profit and a customer for life.

In my business, not all healthcare entities are focused on outcomes the way we are at CAC, and that is a huge problem.

Whether we're talking about Medicare, Medicaid, or the commercial insurance industry, it is a problem that needs to be solved.

———

In most industries, however, success is inevitably predicated upon outcomes.
Our example about the auto repair industry can be overlaid on any situation in which an end user is involved.

———

We can't separate the financial components of an exceptional service experience from the WOW Moment concepts we've been developing, and we wouldn't want to. Business is, after all, business. Customers, clients, and patients don't begrudge the businesses they patronize the opportunity to make money. Let's not hide from it.

Let's also acknowledge how the service experience benefits the profit and loss statement. In our industry, we spend considerable time and money trying to keep our clients healthy. We are very big on healthcare education. We share a regular flow of information with the members of our community on good health practices of all types. We offer classes and seminars in our medical centers on everything from exercise and diet to yoga and nutrition. If you are a senior who lives alone, we will deliver your meals following a hospitalization or transport you to your medical appointments. Our centers provide regular social events that encourage community involvement. Take a class on diabetes or heart care. Play mind and memory games. Dance.

We don't charge for this involvement or for these activities. We're trying to create WOW Moments. We want people to say, "Wow, look what the CAC center offers us. It's special. Why would I go anywhere else for my healthcare needs?"

It should be said that this community involvement and information pipeline are not entirely altruistic.

We want these same people to come to our centers for their health care needs too. We want them to know that the people who offer weekly bingo and daily yoga classes also have the best doctors and nurses around. We want them to know that the same people who offer transportation to their medical appointments also have the most caring medical staff in the business. I call these WOW Moment outcomes.

If we look back on our auto service example, the same approach applies. If your garage offers to shepherd you to and from work after you've dropped off your car, they're going to get your attention. If they top off your transmission fluid for free, they risk setting themselves apart from the competition and getting you to say, "Wow, that was great. They didn't have to do that, but they did."

In our medical centers, it's about a team approach to making the end users feel special and providing them with services and products our competitors can't match. We want it to be as much about our referral staff and our medical assistants as we do our doctors and nurses, and as much about our maintenance department as our corporate office. We want it to be about an entire community. That's powerful. And that's what the WOW Moment concept is all about.

Business is about design. You have to have a clear understanding of the overall service experience, and you have to create an operational design that supports that experience.

This design should include a definition of the WOW Moment outcome. What does success look like in your eyes throughout the organization? For example, I use a very broad definition for what a WOW Moment outcome should look like. And it's simple. I want every single patient who leaves my medical center to understand that we genuinely care for her. That's what success is. Put another way, I don't want even one patient leaving our medical center saying, "I don't know if they really care or not."

From there, I push this definition to my entire team. No, I don't say, "I want 15 people standing by the door saying to 15 patients leaving our facility some morning, 'Do you feel like we care about you here at CAC?'" That would be disingenuous. But I am very clear in making a larger, more broadly based statement that I don't want any one person ever leaving the medical center wondering if my people really get what great healthcare means, or if our organization individually and collectively really cares about him. With that message, our team can then begin to think about experiences that promote that general definition. That's how I want them thinking.

If you're Ford Motor Company, the definition of a WOW Moment outcome might be slightly different. You may see it as a gut emotional response when someone sees a new car come off the line. Something like, "Wow, I've got to have that car." I imagine the CEO of Ford wanting exactly that kind of reaction. Then the "Wow" can go even deeper: "Now that I have the car of my dreams, I want to keep it for a long time because it performs exactly the way I want it to and because it's off-the-charts dependable."

A WOW Moment can be five years into the ownership of this car when you realize how little maintenance it's needed, how great the gas mileage has always been, and how well it's run. "Wow, I did good when I bought this car. I'm a Ford guy (or gal) for life." That's a WOW Moment outcome.

Those are big picture outcomes. What about the small, everyday ones? For example, I want every single person at my front desk to say, "Hi, how are you?" when someone comes through the door. I can insist that there are coffee and small pastries waiting for our guests in every waiting room, and that someone offers them to every patient when she arrives. All good. But that is not the experience we're talking about. That's a service basic. Anyone can match that. Best Buy has a greeter at the front door and so does Wal-Mart. The challenge is to create experiences that go beyond the basics and do so in such a way that it makes it extremely difficult for someone to copy or even match it.

———

Here's the key. WOW Moments are not cosmetic. They can't stand alone from the product or service that you're providing.

———

WOW Moments have to influence the expectations that people have about your product or service in a positive way. Our product, for example, is providing quality medical care that demonstrates a deep caring for our patients. WOW Moments have to maximize this product and make it long lasting. Those are the outcomes that add up to a successful business.

CHAPTER FIFTEEN

It's All About Promoting Action

Picture a billboard.

Picture a patient exiting the doors of a medical center with a smile on her face.

Picture four words in big letters and enclosed by quotes: **"I trust my doctor."**

This is an example of what a CAC ad might look like, be it a billboard or a full page spread in a magazine.

We are in the business of providing the best medical care possible, but we are also in the business of marketing our services. We can't be in business if we're not turning a profit, so a part of our thinking has to take this focus.

―――

We want to retain every patient who walks into our medical centers, and we want people who may never have visited our facilities or been treated by our physicians to give us a try.

―――

Our goal is to get them to take some action: in other words, to decide when a health issue arises to come see us. Then we know that giving them an extraordinary experience will lead them to patronize us every time they need medical care and to advocate for our services out in the community.

Your business is no different. The best airline in the business has two goals: one, to provide a flying experience that nets them a loyal customer base; and two, to influence people who fly with other airlines to give them a try. If they implement the WOW Moment concept, making their customers' flying experience extraordinary – and this could be the added leg room everyone is seeking or the best on-time record in the industry – then that loyal customer base will grow exponentially.

I'm talking here about Southwest Airlines. Remember the funny announcements, the very engaging flight attendants and pilots, and their unusual uniforms? The focus is on creating an experience.

———

In most businesses, the two most important words we can relate to customer relations are emotion and trust.

———

If you're selling widgets, this may be less true than in the healthcare business. But for most businesses in between, an exchange of services and/or products touches both of these essentials: emotion and trust.

Trust equates to predictability. It equates to faith in a customer's primary contact within an organization and, from there, the organization as a whole. When that trust is honored – by delivering a great product or a timely service, for example – there is an emotional response that ties that client or customer that much closer to the organization. The opposite is equally true.

"I trust my doctor" is not just a slogan. If that phrase doesn't generate trust and positive emotion, then the result is the pendulum swinging completely in the opposite direction. That spells trouble for any organization.

If a restaurant serves a regular customer a less than satisfying meal, that customer might give it one more chance before jumping ship. If a new customer is served a less than satisfying meal, he will never return. Trust is about consistency; emotion is the result of exceptional consistency.

If that new customer is blown away by the décor in a restaurant and loves the entrée he orders, you can predict the response. But if the waitress surprises a couple with an after-dinner liqueur courtesy of the house, that positive response will very likely be elevated to a WOW Moment. Now the result is even more emotional. That customer now has something to share at the office the next day, in the form of, "You have to try this new restaurant." Now he has taken action on behalf of the restaurant. And, as we all know, that's the best advertising in the world.

Picture another billboard.

Picture a car pulling up to the entrance to a luxurious hotel and a bellman opening the door for a handsomely dressed couple.

Picture four words in big letters and enclosed by quotes: **"Always Arrive In Style."**

This is how I might imagine a billboard or a full-page ad in *The New Yorker* magazine for, say, BMW.

Melding the photo with the words does two things, hopefully. It conveys class and luxury while at the same time giving the viewer a sense of dependability and reliability. You can't have the former without the latter. The aim of the first half of this equation is to elicit a positive response from a potential buyer, as in: *I want that car; that's my baby.* The second part of the equation is the thing that brings a customer back time and time again, building the kind of loyalty that elicits this kind of response: *I'm a BMW guy (or girl), and I'm proud of it.*

Whether it's CAC or BMW, even a billboard with a photo and four words is built upon establishing a relationship worthy of action. The whole notion of business in general – and in particular the sales and marketing aspects – is to connect. Connecting leads to relationships. Healthy relationships make it infinitely easier for your end user to take action. In our case at CAC, that action relates directly to a patient choosing our medical center over any other healthcare entity in South Florida. In the case of BMW, that action relates directly to a car buyer choosing their brand and their dealerships over Mercedes, Toyota, GM, or Ford. Relationships are key.

As human beings, we want to relate. We want to be involved and respected. We want to take action.

I remember being in my twenties and studying to become a nurse. I was interviewing for a position in a nursing home to build my resume of health-related hours. The gentleman conducting the interview pointed to the books on his bookshelf, and casually commented on his love of reading and the many books that had influenced him over the years. I thought he was making idle conversation instead of trying, as he was, to draw me into a relationship. I missed it completely. I said something to the effect of, "Oh, yeah, yeah, I happen to really like comic books."

Yes, that was my unfortunate reply, but I was too inexperienced to know that he was sizing me up. He was asking himself if I were someone who could fit into his company and embrace the culture he had created. He was running a nursing home and he was testing my ability to relate, not only to him, but to his clientele.

I kept missing the cues, and it cost me an opportunity.

Building relationships is very much about observing those cues, very much about paying attention. You cannot create a WOW Moment if you're not in tune to these relational cues. You have to observe clients, customers, or patients as individuals, connect with who they are as a person, and get in tune with their expectations. What exactly do they expect from your product or service? What do they consider a quality interaction with you and your company, your salespeople, your customer service people, your doctors and nurses, if you will.

———

If you're willing to make a connection and get to know someone, you'll be able to gauge his expectations.
Then, you'll be able to exceed them by creating WOW Moments!

———

For the manager of the local BMW dealership, providing three free oil changes might serve as a WOW Moment for Mr. and Mrs. Jones, while a thank you call from the dealership's owner might be that WOW Moment for a retiree on a pension. The hope is that those free oil changes or the phone call will compel Mr. and Mrs. Jones and our retiree to mention the fine folks at the BMW dealership to a friend or family member and to say, "You can't go wrong there."

From a purely business point of view, this beats trying to get a disgruntled customer back or to induce a new customer to patronize you for the first time solely from a cost perspective. It's all about retention, and there is nothing like a WOW Moment to seal the bonds of a relationship. You've gone above and beyond, and Mr. and Mrs. Jones and our retiree know it.

At our medical centers we actually have a person whose title is Patient Experience Project Manager. This person is accountable for the overall experience that patients have in our centers, from the time they come in the door to the time they leave, and leaving may very well include free transportation to and from their house. The Patient Experience Manager's sole function is to monitor the pluses and minuses of the patient experience and to eliminate as many of the minuses as possible. Her job is to look at the patient experience and to note where we are falling short of organizational goals and customer expectations. If the two are not aligned, changes are made.

———

This is all about taking the verbal and non-verbal cues people are giving off and acting on them.

———

The Patient Experience Manager asks questions of patients waiting in the lobby, studies disenrollment and retention reports, studies every aspect of customer service, holds focus groups, rides transportation buses, and is constantly asking questions and listening to responses. Then it is my job to take those responses and use them to promote action in a positive way.

Healthcare is interesting. Because of governmental regulations you can't offer inducements to customers or potential customers. You can't offer $20 gift cards if someone makes an appointment with one of your doctors. You can't offer a discount on prescriptions to new patients who enroll at your center.

On the other hand, we do offer health-related educational sessions and fitness classes while patients are waiting for an appointment. It may seem like a small thing in some respects, but something as simple as a place to read a magazine, play dominos, and obtain your prescription medications, all in one location, magnifies the community feel of our centers and brings our patients closer together. WOW Moments. Think of an elderly woman with diabetes coming into our center and knowing she can receive a diabetic pedicure before visiting her doctor. Having expanded health-related services is a meaningful way of showing how much her patronage means to us.

The WOW Moment concept focuses on the long term. We want customers who pledge their loyalty because of the services they've received and the quality of the care our doctors and nurses have demonstrated. We want customers who value their relationships with our staff members.

We want a medical center that feels like home, not because of short-term gimmicks, but based upon a quality long-term healthcare experience.

Now we have customers who know exactly where their loyalties lie. Now we have customers ready and willing to take action on our behalf because they have seen the quality of our actions on their behalf.

Taking an experience into the realm of the extraordinary by employing the WOW Moment concept galvanizes your customers and clients to take action. They've seen how much you care. They've found an organization that cares enough about them to go the extra mile. That's what any customers want. They want to do business with someone who genuinely cares about them.

When we talked in the beginning of this chapter about promoting action, the action at the forefront of that statement is the customer's desire to do business with you.

Some WOW Moments are elaborate, like our example earlier in the book of the staff members at one of our medical centers who brought food to a patient's disabled son every day for two weeks. Others are simple, like taking a patient's hands and assuring her that we will be doing everything in our power to get her well.

But the one thing all WOW Moments do – big or small, simple or elaborate - is get people to take action, and most often your business is the beneficiary.

CHAPTER SIXTEEN

One Shoe Does Not Fit All

When I arrived at CAC, I was determined to change the culture. We were a top-down organization. Everything revolved around the corporate office. It was the place to be. Being in the corporate office was a sign of success.

You can imagine the turmoil that the WOW Moment concept first caused for the 800 or so people who were so used to doing it the other way. "What? Wait! You mean we're now going to put our medical centers and the services we offer there first? You mean we're going to focus our energies on making the patient experience the most important thing on our agenda?"

Yes. And yes. And what's more, we're going to focus on making that experience extraordinary. We're going to go beyond the expectations of our customers and create moments that cause them to say, "Wow! That was special. These people really care."

This was, for our company, revolutionary thinking. Not everyone bought in.

Never assume everyone will buy in.

Picture your company. You run a large printing company. Volume has always been king. Now you go to your annual meeting, and you announce a change in direction that emphasizes the WOW Moment concept. It sounds pretty darn good when you start explaining the long-term implications of exceeding your customers' expectations. Some of your salespeople don't buy in. They make their money with big orders and fast turnover. They don't see things two or three years down the road, because they might not even be in your employ in two or three years. How do you deal with it?

With my team, I naturally had similar issues. I remember very clearly the problems that surfaced with three doctors in particular who simply did not buy into the relevancy of the overall experience. Their attitudes were simple: Get the patient in and out of the office as quickly as possible. Go home, grab your golf clubs, and get in a leisurely nine holes before the sun goes down.

That's not what I had in mind. What's more, our Patient Experience Project Manager concluded that we were losing patients to our competition because of this attitude. These were not bad doctors by any means, but we were taking a different approach to our business and they needed to get onboard or find another place to ply their trade.

The WOW Moment concept requires first and foremost an understanding of what it means to turn an experience into something extraordinary.

It makes perfect sense to some people. For others, including these doctors, it requires training. They didn't understand the philosophy behind putting the end user first, and they couldn't conceptualize a WOW Moment. Like sitting down with an 80-year-old woman with diabetes and asking her about her grandchildren. Like spending five minutes with a cancer patient and discussing his favorite books. Laughing at someone's joke. Giving someone a hug.

The three doctors in question either didn't believe in exceptional bedside manners or had none. I didn't blame them. But they had to be retrained. This was our new culture. We were moving in a patient-first direction. One of the doctors embraced our WOW Moment training and admitted to me later that it gave his career a new lease on life. One didn't have the personality for it and transferred to another position. The third refused to budge and was let go. He didn't have the discipline or the rigor to know where the company needed to go and what levels of service were required to get us there. What's even more important was that he was turning patients into detractors of our company.

As a leader, you need to know what you will accept in terms of your team's behavior and what you will not accept.

Given the results with these three doctors, and given the fact that the WOW Moment concept is not meant for everyone, I considered the process a success in this example.

The owner of the print shop faces the same challenges.

He has to convince his staff that the company's service basic is not enough over the long haul. He has to convince his staff that giving their customers an exceptional experience is best for everyone. It will insure the loyalty of long-term customers and convince short-term and new customers that they've found a printer who really cares about getting their order right. That's what makes long-term customers, and long-term customers bode well for job security.

If he has salesmen on staff who don't see the big picture and don't buy in, then he faces retraining them – and a good salesman is probably worth the effort – or making a change.

Cultural changes within an organization are huge. The enormity sometimes convinces a leader that it's not worth it. From my perspective, however, change is a necessary component in running any business, and a good leader knows that the status quo only works for so long. If nothing else, a cultural change gives employees a new perspective and a new burst of energy. And if the change works to the degree that the WOW Moment concept has worked for us, everyone prospers, including the customer.

Evaluating the customer experience begins with a study of all the possible touch points between a company's associates and its customers, or, in our case at CAC, between our staff and our patients. These touch points are universal. If you're in business, there are key points of interaction between your customers and your employees. And these touch points are crucial in searching for areas where the WOW Moment concept fits.

Where does it begin? What is the first touch point? This is crucial, because it sets the tone of all interactions to come.

If a patient receives a rude response when he or she calls to schedule an appointment, the experience is already off to a bad start; you've already failed with a service basic. How can you create an exceptional experience when you've slammed the door on it before it ever begins?

If the receptionist at the medical center where the patient has made his or her appointment is staring down at her smartphone when they arrive, we have a similar problem. You can't create a WOW Moment if you don't start by observing the most basic service of all:

a simple, enthusiastic greeting. That's one of the first touch points on our list.

But there are many: when the bus picks up a patient for a ride to the clinic; the waiting room; first contact with a nurse; first contact with a doctor; the referral department; the lab department. The list goes on. We value every touch point, and we discuss possible WOW Moments that exceed a patient's expectations when it comes to these touch points. We talk about cause and effect, both short term and long term. We practice. We see how good it feels when a patient says, "Wow. I didn't expect that."

Touch points are not individual moments. Each touch point influences the next one. It's very difficult to erase a rude reception by a nurse with a warm one by a doctor. Consistency is key. And that's why you don't ignore any touch point. They're all important.

For the printer we were talking about, it begins with a call from a salesperson. Can you imagine if that salesperson hasn't bought into the WOW Moment concept? Let's just say that the potential for a positive, long-term relationship is behind the eight-ball right from the outset.

In our home state of Florida, where it's hot and muggy a good part of the time, we make sure our buses are air conditioned. This is good for the patient and his family to be sure. It's also good for the bus driver whose job it is to be ultra courteous and ultra helpful; this is a lot easier if the bus he is driving for eight hours is comfortable.

We make certain the people manning our appointment desks are prepared with procedures that enhance every interaction; we don't leave this to chance. And then we walk them through the WOW Moment concept so that they understand what it means to make an experience extraordinary.

The question we ask from one touch point to another is this: How do we create an interaction that shows our end user that we care? We want all our people asking: Did I miss an opportunity for a WOW Moment? I want these two questions to influence the behaviors of everyone from the maintenance department to the office of the CEO.

I mentioned training your associates. Even more important is empowering your associates.

It is your job to help your associates understand what's important to your organization. It is your job to make sure they understand what the customer experience needs to look like. But most important is empowering them to deliver on that.

Remember the story we told earlier about the man who took his family on a Disney cruise? His son was so disappointed when they missed the breakfast event featuring all the Disney characters. Fortunately, the event's hostess saw an opportunity for a WOW Moment and had Mickey and Minnie, in full costume, visit the little boy in person the next morning.

The hostess understood the Disney culture that mandated an "end user first" mentality, one built upon understanding the customer experience and making that experience extraordinary whenever possible. She was also empowered to make that happen on her own.

This all relates back to the hiring process. You start with people who are positive. You start with people who see work as more than just a job. You start with people who are predisposed to the WOW Moment concept, see its value, and understand that they can get as much out of the experience as the customer can. In other words, hire for attitude and train for skill!

Once hired, these very special people are trained to understand the customer experience and the importance of the "end user first" philosophy. They learn how to identify customer expectations and what it means to exceed those expectations. They are trained to identify WOW Moment opportunities and how to make them real. Lastly, they are trained to manage the whole customer (or patient) experience and to understand how the results of this lead to a more productive, profitable company.

You add value to the workplace. You make work a more enjoyable, rewarding situation.

This reflects directly on the customer (or patient) experience, and it makes your company a more desirable place to do business.

The WOW Moment concept is not for everyone. It is not a one-shoe-fits-all approach to doing business. Some people won't get it. Some people will fight it. But once you share the concept, most employees find it energizing. And all it takes is providing one customer, client, or patient with a WOW Moment to see the extraordinary effect it has on them. And all it takes is one WOW Moment to see how positively it affects the employee responsible for it.

It may not be a one-shoe-fits-all culture, but it is a culture that provides a win for everyone involved.

CHAPTER SEVENTEEN

WOW Moments Leave Nothing to Chance

When your goal is a workplace environment predicated upon the idea of taking the customer experience and making it extraordinary, you cannot leave anything to chance or to assumption. You really can't. When you are talking about exceeding customer expectations and going beyond the service basic, it is not a hit or miss proposition.

When you are defining the overall customer experience, you have to be clear and definitive.

The entire team, from the C-Suite to the factory floor – or in our case at CAC, to the associates who man our medical centers 24/7 – has to have an unbiased understanding of what the WOW Moment concept is. If anyone on your team is making things up as he goes along, then he has missed the boat. And so have you as a leader.

This does not mean that everyone on your team is walking around with a list of potential WOW Moments spelled out for him like the ingredients of a recipe. Not at all. WOW Moments are very often improvised or conjured up on the fly. If one of our nurses sees a patient struggling to make a phone call on his cell phone because he forgot his reading glasses – yes, this happens all the time with the aging population we see in our centers – she doesn't have a pre-rehearsed WOW Moment just for the occasion. She has to understand what it means to take this experience and make it special. What if she walks up to this patient with a smile and says, "Who are we trying to reach this afternoon, sir? Why don't you let me give you a hand." Maybe she helps this patient input the phone number and takes him to an area where he'll have some privacy. Or maybe the nursing staff keeps a couple of pairs of magnifying reading glasses handy just for such occasions.

  Whatever the answer, if this nurse understands and embraces the idea of turning experience into extraordinary, then the WOW Moment will materialize on the spot. She'll know that there is no service basic for helping a patient make a phone call, but she'll see an opportunity to make a patient feel comfortable and special because she gets the concept. Why? Because the culture we have declared at CAC includes in-depth training on exactly what the concept is and how it can change the patient experience.

———

In a culture that embraces the WOW Moment concept, we don't leave anything to chance.

———

If you happen to be running a school that teaches adult immigrants how to speak English, you can set up a dozen classrooms with posters on the walls and desks with hard, wooden seats, just like so many classrooms in schools all over the country. You can go page by page through the recommended textbook. Or, you can conduct your classes in live settings around the city and allow your students to experience their new language in the real world, where it really counts.

Yes, you use the prescribed text books, just like we play soothing music in our buses and make sure the televisions in our waiting areas are showing positive, health-related programs, and that the posters in our examinations rooms have a health-conscious message. But those are service basics. The question for the English language teacher is how to bring the language to life so all of her students are having fun with it, so that they go home after class and say, "Wow, I'm really learning something."

I don't believe in overkill when it comes to the overall experience. I don't believe you can be over-prepared in defining the patient experience desired.

For example, we have three "greeters" in the lobby of each of our centers. I never want a patient to enter the lobby and not have the full attention of one of our greeters. And our greeters aren't there solely to say hello. They are there to direct our patients, offer a helping hand with bags or wheelchairs, and to make sure the patient is fully apprised of each and every aspect of his visit. "Be present" is a mandate for every person in our centers whenever they are "on stage."

If, for example, a patient has forgotten one of her labs, the greeter's job is to find out where that particular report is coming from and make sure it's in her doctor's file the moment she steps into an examination room. That is getting to the experience and elevating it well beyond the basics.

Imagine our English language school providing transportation for students who may not have access to a car, or who may have missed their bus for some reason. That's a WOW Moment.

There is a fine line between telling your staff exactly what to do and making certain that everyone is aware of the customer's expectation. We don't lay out every move our associates make; that doesn't allow them to do their jobs with a sense of ownership. We expect there to be soothing music in the reception area of our centers, but we don't have a scripted greeting that our greeters are expected to use in welcoming a patient and her family.

In every Apple retail store around the country, the interior designs are very clean lined and very predictable. The tables are identical. The colors are neutral. Why? Because they want you and me to focus on the material on each of the tables and to see only the equipment hanging from the walls. Everything has a purpose. The help desk is located at the rear of the store, because they want you and me to walk past every product in the store to get there. Everything is by design. Nothing is left to chance.

It's an experience going into an Apple store. The staff wear identical shirts that clearly identify them as Apple associates. And these associates know their products inside and out. But what they know even better is the Apple customer. They know that the Apple customers and their needs have been at the forefront of Apple product development, and the associate treats the customer accordingly. That is what elevates the experience. You're not a number; you're an Apple advocate.

The culture that you create in your company has to be purposeful. It can't evolve from an assumption, and it can't just happen.

A culture, like a business strategy, is not open to interpretation. That is why it is so important that the man or woman at the top clearly and succinctly spells it out. "This is our purpose. This is the direction we will take to achieve that purpose." It is the job of the man or woman at the top of any organization, big or small, to define why the company exists and to do so in a way that is positive and forthright.

A huge part of my job at CAC is to make certain that all of our associates – from the C-suite and our medical staff, to our medical center associates from the top of the organizational chart to the bottom – understand our mission and are clear about our vision: we all serve our patients. Our mission is to help every person in every community we serve to achieve lifelong well-being. Period. End of statement. Clear and straightforward.

Part two of my role is to achieve a "buy in" from every person on my team. This means getting out and pounding the pavement, making contact, listening.

The WOW Moment culture takes some explaining. It takes setting an example. It takes enthusiasm that no one can possibly mistake for anything less than total commitment. If I'm not in 110%, then it's all for naught.

Whatever culture you establish as the leader of your organization is not up for debate, and you can't just issue a memo and expect results. You, as the leader of your organization, have to be the very best representative of your culture. Your team has to see it in action every time you step out the door.

At CAC, we are a goal-oriented organization with very definable results, and I hold everyone accountable for those results, starting with me. There's an end goal, and everyone knows what that is: we want our patients to be as healthy as they can be, we want them to be happy, and we want them to stay with us over the long haul. These are our goals.

If I can't create at least one tangible WOW Moment every day, then I am not doing my part as the leader of the culture I have created.

We've all heard the saying: people don't know what they don't know. A cliché perhaps, but one with an enormous amount of truth to it. In short, you have to build your culture into the everyday work environment and immerse your people into the very fabric of that culture. A person can't act on something he or she hasn't been informed about and trained to understand and implement. A culture takes on meaning when it becomes ingrained in the psyche of the organization and every member: This is how we do things. Here is the strategy. Here is the language we intend to use. Here are the symbols that represent our culture.

You don't get that message across via email. You get it across with a level of communication that knocks people off their feet. You get it by getting out of the office and making your presence felt on the factory floor (whatever your "factory floor" happens to look like). You get it by creating WOW Moments that resonate long after you're gone. "Wow, did she really spend an entire day with a shovel in her hand?" "Wow, did he really come down here and help us rearrange our files?"

You state your purpose, you provide direction, and you motivate. None is more or less important than the other.

How does your culture look? How will you implement it? What are the results you expect?

If I walk into one of my medical centers and ask one of my associates to tell me about a WOW Moment that she produced today, and she says, "What's a WOW Moment?" then I've failed as a leader.

Communication has to be purposeful and very well thought out, but the frequency of your message has to be consistent as well. So does your follow up. So does the language that you use, and the symbols that represent your culture.

Nothing in leadership is by chance.

I believe that every company is founded on some belief. If you hold true to that belief, it becomes that heritage piece that your company carries forward year after year. The medical centers at CAC were, for example, founded upon a one-stop shop model where all of a patient's needs are satisfied, from diagnosis to treatment to follow up. If a model is sound, it begins with a set of values that eventually generate traditions that everyone can identify with. In our case, we are going to treat everyone like family. That's our heritage. I didn't change that when I became the company CEO. I had to figure out how best to acknowledge that identity and to make it even more viable. That's how I see the WOW Moment concept.

Nothing enhances a relationship like a WOW Moment, something that shows how much you truly care. Whether it's at home or in the workplace, WOW Moment behaviors allow a patient, a spouse, or a customer to see just how much they mean to you. You went the extra mile. You turned an experience into extraordinary. And in doing so, you go all the way back to the belief that has been driving your organization from the get-go. You reinforce the values that serve as the foundation for your actions.

Nothing is by chance.

CHAPTER EIGHTEEN

Honoring the Past to Affect the Future

The past influences the present, which inspires what is to come in the future. That is an underlying component of the WOW Moment philosophy.

If you intend for a personal relationship to be successful over the long term, it behooves you to respect your partner's past, does it not? No matter what path people have traveled, that journey completely influences where they are today and will unmistakably impact where they are going, which means it must irrevocably influence their relationship with you.

———

I don't believe you can discount a person's past and still have a positive future together; that defies human nature.

———

Evolution, change, and growth are almost always a good thing, but to discount the impact past events, past relationships, and past behaviors have on that evolution, change, and growth is not in line with the WOW Moment concept.

The very same dynamics are true in business as well. The traditions created by past leaders are irrevocably interwoven in the fabric of an organization, and they have to be honored before moving forward. The legacy left by current and previous employees is what gives an organization its bones, if you will, and discarding this heritage is counterproductive.

Amazingly, this happens all the time. A new management team will come in and want to clean house, top to bottom, traditions and legacy be damned. How often do you see a new CEO come into an organization and demonize his or her predecessor, followed by, "And now I, your knight in shining armor, am going to save you from all the missteps of those really average people who came before me."

This "knight in shining armor" mentality rarely works. Yes, the goal of every employee in an organization, from top to bottom, should be lifting the organization to the next level. Nothing wrong with that mentality. Nothing wrong with saying, "What we've built is good, but now how can we do more and do it better?" That is a positive statement. You revere tradition and heritage in the process, even as you begin to tweak them with an eye on the organization's growth and evolution. What you don't do is scrap those traditions or vilify the legacy.

Even if a company is in trouble, as it often is when an entirely new management is installed, you respect the foundational aspects of the business. Even if you turn a company around, you must respect the past.

I was extremely proud of my team and our organization when we grew revenues by 28% in my first year and cut costs by 22%, making it one of the most profitable years CAC had ever experienced. We began, however, by honoring the heritage and traditions of the whole organization and a past that had a 50-year history. Then we let our actions speak for us.

That is what the WOW Moment culture signifies: a respect for the past with a focus on the present and an eye on the future. We are concerned about a patient's experience today while looking for ways to turn that experience into something exceptional in the future.

Too many businesses are willing to forfeit the long term for the sake of short-term gains when in fact, the two are irrevocably tied together. We want our patients leaving our medical centers as healthy as possible, not just sort of healthy, so they'll be back sooner. If they leave our centers feeling great, we know they'll look to us for their healthcare needs down the road because we did great work today. Mediocre service gets people back in the short term out of pure necessity, but it will have them looking elsewhere over the long haul.

A stockbroker who pushes a mediocre investment opportunity on a client for the sake of a commission today will likely lose that client later, when she realizes the broker was putting his own best interest in front of hers. Steering the client away from that mediocre investment could have been a WOW Moment; instead, it was an opportunity missed.

———

I know one thing from my many years in business. People want to be a part of something special. How we win together is a mutually shared idea. That's what it is.

———

People want to buy in. People want to connect. People want to participate in something impactful and meaningful.

You may have heard the saying: "Success has many fathers and failure is a bastard."

I'm sure there are many interpretations of these nine words, but I think this saying means that people want to be a part of the winning team. People want to pick the winning team. The embryonic stage of this is the recognition of shared values.

As a leader, you begin by creating a team of people who represent your values and the values that you see as the foundational components for your organization moving forward.

These values represent your business and all that it stands for. In a very real sense, they represent who you are as the leader of this organization. No, you're not looking for clones. No, you're not looking for "yes" men or "yes" women. You're looking for people who can respect the vision of the organization. You're looking for people who get excited by the culture you're espousing. You're looking for people who can take the ball and run with it, knowing they understand the purpose and direction you've laid out for the organization.

I don't want people to think that the goal is to create the same WOW Moments that I would create for our patients. I want people who embrace the WOW Moment philosophy and feel excited about getting out there and creating their own WOW Moments.

The owner of an advertising company doesn't hire a visual artist who designs exactly like she does or sees their clients exactly as she sees them. She doesn't want someone with the exact same aesthetic or a world view that mirrors her own. Instead, she hires someone with talent, vision, and enthusiasm, someone who also understands the culture driving the firm and respects the traditions that have gotten the firm where it is today.

I call this a shared value. In the culture I've created at CAC, this shared value is directly related to the experience of our end user and a commitment to making that experience extraordinary. Just getting the job done doesn't fit this shared value. Caring about the mark you make in the world does fit it.

Every company has to evolve, even in the face of the heritage and traditions of the past. But the minute that evolution shuns the values that drive the company, it's a lost cause.

Does the owner of the advertising company want her new hire to be innovative and aggressively demonstrate his or her talent? Of course. But if that innovation gets in the way of a longstanding value structure that, say, was built around a respect for the client's ideas, then the owner has hired the wrong person.

The WOW Moment concept will never thrive in an organization where the employees view their job simply as a means of generating income. It won't work. The job has to be a calling; it must be meaningful to them.

If I were to ever hear one of my associates say, "They don't pay me enough to care," then I know the WOW Moment concept is a lost cause for them.

Caring and WOW Moments go hand in hand. That's what makes the concept so special and so viable.

You have to be fully present in your calling to create WOW Moments. Let's go back to our example about the newly hired visual artist at our advertising firm. Imagine her walking into a consultation with her very first client, say, the owner of a chain of local coffee houses doing battle with the nationwide brands we're all familiar with. Imagine her shaking hands with her client and saying, "I just have to tell you how much I respect the business you've built and the guts it takes to go up against the likes of larger national competitor chains. I really admire that."

Some people might see this as fawning or sucking up; I call it a WOW Moment. I call it a way of stepping away from what is expected and creating a special interaction. I can hear the client saying, "Wow, that was unexpected," and being grateful for the recognition. What's more, this new hire has fully respected the history and culture created by her client.

When I first came on board at CAC, there was always an empty chair in every meeting I presided over, no matter how big or small. That chair belonged to our patient, and it took center stage in every discussion we ever had. In fact, if someone veered off track, I would very politely stop him, point to the chair, and say, "We started wrong. Let's go back and address concern #1, the patient's needs."

While the empty chair was only a prop I used in the beginning of my tenure, it was meant to clarify the values I wanted us to be honoring and to emphasize the cultural shift I was advocating. And that's the point. No matter what industry you're in or the size of your enterprise, there has to be a value system upon which the foundation of your business is based and a culture that spells out very clearly what you stand for. In our case at CAC, an empty chair in a meeting was simply a symbol that reinforced this.

———

The addition of the WOW Moment concept to our way of doing business would not have been possible if our "culture of service" had not been established from day one.

———

The good news about the WOW Moment concept is that it's very hard to argue against. Making the customer experience special resonates with anyone who understands that you won't be in business for long if you don't honor the people who buy your product or service.

Being in business is more than earning a living. It's about the customers who spend their money supporting our business. Therefore, it follows rather naturally that making the customer's experience extraordinary can only aid in our quest to do more than earn a living.

Being in business is also all about making a difference. I know this sounds cliché, but that doesn't make it any less true.

I look at CAC and am proud of the jobs we provide; more than that, I think we're providing our associates with a chance to make a difference in their own right, servicing our patients' healthcare needs and, most importantly, taking their healthcare experience to a level our competition can't match.

Making a difference doesn't have to be earth shattering. WOW Moments don't have to be earth shattering. Giving your customers a little something extra can make their day, it can make your day, and it doesn't have to cost anything. It feels good going home after work knowing you've made someone feel good about his or her day.

You give a client two tickets to the baseball game.

You plant a tree in a customer's name.

You stop to help a disabled customer struggling to make a call.

You remember the birthday of a client's son or daughter.

These are WOW Moments. They represent a step beyond your clients' normal expectations. It takes their experience to a new level. And very likely, experiencing a WOW Moment, they will pay it forward. Now you've created a ripple effect within your community.

CHAPTER NINETEEN

Improvisation and the WOW Moment

"Seek first to understand, then to be understood."

Too often, men and women who serve in some kind of managerial or supervisory position get this wrong. Their goal is to make damn sure that the people answering to them, answer to them exactly the way they want them to. How often do we encounter this type of management approach? "Do it this way!" Or, just as misguided, "Don't do it this way." You might as well say, "We have a script – which I wrote - and I want you to stick with it no matter what." This may empower the supervisor, but it does nothing toward empowering the person in the trenches.

―――――

I'm convinced that empowering your employees is a better way to approach a conversation.

―――――

I start by saying, "Help me understand why you approached the work this way." This is, first and foremost, non-threatening. Second of all, it opens the door to a meaningful conversation and creates a dialogue. This is empowering, on the one hand; on the other, it gives me an opportunity to gain insight into a way of thinking I may not have considered.

If I say to one of my staff, "You went off script, and I want to know why," I have now put him on the defensive. Most importantly, if I come off like it's my way or the highway, I may very well miss a learning opportunity.

A good leader cannot afford to stop learning; I know this sounds like a cliché, but it amazes me how often someone is elevated to a position of authority, and his growth ceases.

And here's the thing. If you've already established an organizational culture – in our case at CAC, the WOW Moment culture that puts the best interest of our customers front and center – then anything that aids or expands that culture is a good thing.

Most leaders say they want to empower their people to think for themselves, even if it means approaching goals or solving problems in ways that might not follow company script to the letter. The question is, do they really mean it?

For me, it's a learning experience. Maybe this unconventional or out-of-the-box approach needs to be examined more closely and shared with other people in the organization. Maybe first understanding the tactics, approaches, and behaviors that we see in others can lead to bigger and better things and a better understanding of ourselves.

So it really IS about listening and learning.

When I see something that seems off script, unconventional, or innovative, I like to say, "So help me understand why you did it that way and then from there let's measure the results."

Here's a WOW Moment example:

Our centers are in South Florida. For years, we served coffee in the morning to patients coming in early. We always served these bite-sized treats we called pastelitos along with the coffee. Pastelitos are really nothing more than tiny pastries. In the northeast, they fill them with chicken or beef. Down south, we sweeten them with guava. They're very tasty. However, the problem with pastelitos filled with guava is that they are very sweet. If you happen to be diabetic, which a lot of our patients are, or have a low tolerance for sweets, which a lot of our patients do, then pastelitos flavored with guava may have way too much sugar in them.

One of our receptionists heard a complaint or two about this and responded to the problem by bringing in small fruit cups as an alternative. However, no one knew that she was buying the fruit out of her own pocket and chopping up the fruit before she came to work in the morning to make sure it was fresh.

The fruit cups were an immediate success. Before long, they were trumping the pastelitos as the snack of choice with our early arrivals.

I happened to be in the center one morning and noticed what was going on. I asked one of our greeters where the fruit cups were coming from, and she told me the story. I then approached the receptionist responsible for the fruit cups and asked her about it.

To be honest, I think at first she thought she was in some kind of trouble. After I assured her quite the opposite was true, she went on to explain how the idea had come about and how she got started after having a discussion with the medical director of the center about health and nutrition.

"I think I brought in 15 cups the first day, and they went like wildfire," she said. "So I made twice as many the next day."

"What do you mean, you made them?"

Now I think she thought I was crazy, because she said, "You know, I bought the fruit and cut them up. I also bought some paper cups, which made the perfect portion. Now I bring in 30 or so when I can, and they're perfect with coffee. Our patients love them."

"You've been buying fruit out of your own pocket?"

That she took this initiative was most certainly a WOW Moment for me.

It was also a WOW Moment for the patients who experienced this special treat every morning.

Moreover, I could see that both my reaction and the reaction of our patients made her feel good about the job she was doing. When I said, "That's wonderful. That you'd think of our patients like that and go out of your way for them," she replied, "Well, they deserve it."

I was blown away. She got it. Taking the experience and making it extraordinary.

"I think we should try this at our other centers. Would you like to be in charge of the pilot program?"

"Wow. Really? I sure would."

So from then on, all of our medical centers started serving fresh fruit cups in the morning, and we've actually cut back on the small pastries. Does it cost more? Yes, it does. Fresh fruit costs considerably more than those little pastries do, but now the patient experience is that much better and our patients are that much healthier.

Our receptionist went off script. She thought out of the box. She saw an opportunity to create any number of WOW Moments, and took the initiative to do so.

For my part, I got out of the office and saw something special going on in one of our centers. I stopped, listened, and learned. We recognized the actions of one of our staff, we celebrated it, and we acted on a simple but brilliant idea. Then we implemented the idea across all of the medical centers.

That first morning, one patient came in, saw a fresh fruit cup, and enjoyed it along with his coffee. He said to the receptionist, "Wow, that's special. Thank you," and it is now part of the all-encompassing experience.

One element that I try to emphasize with my staff, and that you as a business owner and leader must recognize, is that customer expectations are fluid.

They could very easily be based upon the kind of day that customer has had. People have mood swings. A hundred things might affect their emotions and their thinking throughout the course of a day. Your company still has a service basic that forms a baseline for you and your staff's interaction with that customer, no matter what her frame of mind. You still have an understanding of what your customer's expectations are, and this doesn't really change just because someone is in a bad mood. You still have an understanding of what it means to move that experience beyond those expectations, though your efforts might not be recognized each and every time.

If a patient comes into our center and the special fruit cups that we offer him don't produce a WOW Moment, that doesn't mean that we are now going to give him a fruit cup and a twenty-dollar bill. It means we are going to respect each and every person and whatever frame of mind he might be in. It means we are still going to be looking for ways to make the experience in our centers exceptional. And maybe the man who comes in sporting a bad mood will leave feeling more upbeat because of a concerted effort by one of our staff to make him laugh. And maybe it means that the woman who came in feeling depressed about her health will leave feeling more optimistic because a nurse or a doctor took the time to fully address her concerns, to reassure her about the treatment she is receiving and the results she could expect.

What I do know is that every unique set of circumstances is a unique opportunity to exceed a customer's expectations and to create a WOW Moment.

If I take my car in to the dealership that I patronize for an oil change and a tune-up, I'm confident that they will do a good job in general, but my expectations are going to vary every time I go in based upon any number of factors. If my son and I had a great breakfast and meaningful conversation before I left the house, I'm probably going to be a pretty easy customer to satisfy. If I'm coming from my office after a less than successful meeting, I might not be in the best of moods, and it's going to take a bit more from the dealership's staff to make my experience extraordinary. But a smile and a pleasant greeting go a long way. The mechanic saying, "We'll make sure everything is running great, Mr. Kent," is even better. And then when I return and realize they've given the inside and outside of my car a thorough cleaning, I have to say, "Wow, I didn't expect that."

    We're all human. Our customers are all human. Our notions of what makes the cut as a WOW Moment might vary from time to time. Still, it is because we are all human that the WOW Moment concept is so effective. We all love it when someone treats us with courtesy and respect. We all love it when someone goes above and beyond on our behalf. That's special. We gravitate naturally to people who treat us with courtesy and respect and we are loyal to a fault to people who go the extra mile on our behalf. That is the heart and soul of the WOW Moment.

Because we're all human, WOW Moments require a certain amount of improvisation.

Because we're all a bit fickle at times and can be unpredictable every so often, no two WOW Moments are ever exactly the same. When you're well versed in the WOW Moment concept, however, you can use this unpredictable human side to your advantage. Just like the guys at the car dealership did when I arrived at their shop in a grouchy mood.

They went beyond the service basic, recognized the customer experience, and then recognized an opportunity to make the experience memorable. All they got in return was a customer for life. Not a bad deal.

CHAPTER TWENTY

Attitude and the WOW Moment

Success is a matter of perception.

Every customer perceives a successful experience with your company differently. That may seem like an uphill battle when you're trying to establish an appropriate connection with every person you encounter in the course of a day, but there is actually good news here.

Let's say you're the owner of a sandwich shop, and Mrs. Jones is your most difficult, finicky customer. Impossible to please, seemingly. She comes in complaining about the weather, even on the most beautiful day, and lets you know right off that you've either got the heat up too high or the air conditioning on too low. Then she begins to question how fresh your bread is and where your tomatoes were grown.

How are you supposed to evaluate the customer experience with someone like Mrs. Jones and then elevate it to something exceptional? The answer is simple really. She will tell you.

The customers know what success looks like to them, and they will always tell you, if you're listening.

For Mrs. Jones, maybe the answer is to take the initiative and tell her right off that the tomatoes you just got in are from a local farm producer and the sweetest things on the planet. Invite her to taste a sample and then serve it with a piece of fresh bread and a cold drink.

The point, of course, is that every customer is an individual, and part of the WOW Moment concept is realizing that every person has his own perception of what your business can offer him. It is this perception of success that requires your attention.

At our medical centers, we do have certain "scripted" items on our agenda. We insist that every customer receive a certain type of greeting. We insist that every waiting room offer certain amenities. We insist that all information relevant to a patient's medical circumstances be conveyed in a certain manner. We train each and every one of our associates in certain protocols with regard to customer service. But we also train them to think for themselves regarding their interaction with patients and to think on their feet when it comes to potential WOW Moments.

I want the members of our team to understand our policies and procedures, but I also want them to take ownership of their customer interaction.

I want them to fully understand the WOW Moment concept and to be empowered to think out of the box when it comes to making the customer experience extraordinary. Part of my conversation with our associates regarding WOW Moment opportunities goes something like this: If you listen, customers will always tell you how they feel, what they expect, what they are hoping for, and what their definition of success is.

One of the first rules in sales is this: You don't really "sell" your customer anything as much as you provide her a "solution." Why? Because the customer knows what she wants or believes she knows what she wants. The salesman's job is to find out the real problem and offer a solution.

Sometimes it may look as if you can't get to a WOW Moment or to a place where the customer's expectations can realistically be exceeded. This cannot, however, be used as an excuse. Sometimes that solution grows from the service basic that you and your firm have established. The best you may be able to offer is an enthusiastic greeting or a warm smile, but you don't allow the circumstances or the situation to determine your efforts.

In the case of my company, patients coming into our medical centers generally know what they are there for. A medical center isn't like a Staples or the Apple Store, where impulse buying is often a factor. In a medical center, a patient comes in wanting treatment for some ailment, rehab for some injury, or a follow up to some previous treatment.

―――

In certain situations, it may seem as if a WOW Moment is neither possible nor perhaps even called for, but this is rarely the case.

―――

A patient has cancer. A woman's husband has died. A child is terminal. It may be that the best our staff can do is show they care, demonstrate empathy, or simply be gentle in their conversation and interaction. I count these as part of our service basic. But the WOW Moment in these cases can often be judged by the sincerity of someone's effort. In such cases as these, the wife who lost her husband might not recognize the sincerity of a nurse's words or the gentleness of her touch until later. When she needs to come in for grief counseling later and realizes there was something special about the interaction she experienced at our center, then she might think: "That was genuine. That was more than I expected."

―――――

All WOW Moments have an element of sincerity in them. They don't have to be serious, however, just genuine.

―――――

If we look back at our sandwich shop example, we suggested that the staff might break through some of Mrs. Jones's negativity by engaging her before she starts criticizing the freshness of the vegetables by offering her a taste of the newly arrived tomatoes. But if the staff's only goal is to placate Mrs. Jones, she'll know. At some level, she'll know. But if they're sincere and genuine in their efforts, then they have a chance of creating a WOW Moment.

The triggers we talked about are always there; you just have to be sincere in finding them. It's all about attitude. And the crazy part about a positive attitude is that it has a boomerang effect. It not only rubs off on your customers, it makes your job more enjoyable.

The one thing I can testify to is that WOW Moments feed off of one another. The fruit cups that we began offering to our patients in the morning have led us to consider bite-sized tuna and chicken salad sandwiches during the noon hour. Healthy and simple. The effect is twofold. One, the offerings invariably get a positive response from our patients. Two, they also serve as a reminder to our patients to think healthy. When a patient tells the receptionist in the waiting room or the nurse in the examination room that he's trying to eat healthier because he sees the kind of food we make available in our center, it's a WOW Moment in reverse.

One of the most effective ways to influence attitude is to recognize the efforts of your team and to celebrate the results. At CAC, we have made this a component within our growth and retention program that we call "Recognize and Celebrate." We've made it into policy that everyone is aware of and everyone understands. Praising in public goes a long way toward raising the morale of your staff. We do this primarily with our in-house quarterly newsletter and with our biannual patient newsletter. We tell stories, we note patient successes, we recognize staff input, we praise innovation, and we celebrate efforts that clearly go above and beyond.

We highlight the efforts of the individual, but we also go out of our way to praise teamwork and departmental successes.

For me, however, newsletters only go so far. I'm a big believer in recognizing effort face-to-face, with a kind word, a pat on the back, and a "well done." I'm a hands-on leader. I want my managers to be hands-on leaders. We all spend a lot of hours at our jobs. A job, as we have said throughout this book, is far more rewarding when it becomes a calling, and the recognition that one receives can go a long way in solidifying that calling.

On the other hand, I don't want the members of my team searching for ways to create a WOW Moment simply to be recognized for their efforts or to be celebrated for their accomplishments. It can't work that way. Most WOW Moments are between one employee and one customer. They are about one person making the customer experience extraordinary.

Yes, the story about the receptionist who introduced the fruit cups to the morning ritual at our centers was written up in our newsletter, but the WOW Moment one of our nurses created when she brought a single rose to everyone during their in-home visit wasn't. The patient newsletter talked about the doctor who volunteered to sponsor and coach a neighborhood soccer team, but made no mention of a center associate who drove an infirm patient to her granddaughter's dance recital and then took them both out for an ice cream cone after it was over. Those are WOW Moments. Two of them were recognized. All of them were celebrated, if only by the people involved.

———

The beauty of Recognize and Celebrate is the ripple effect it often causes.

———

The story about the fruit cups influenced a dozen ideas about how we could improve the customer experience. One far-reaching idea rendered an entirely new in-house physical therapy program and facility. The physician who made this suggestion wasn't expecting to see her picture on the front page of the company newsletter. She saw it as a way to improve our services. You can imagine the number of WOW Moments this new facility has generated for our patients. You can also imagine how our business profited, but that's what happens when the end users in any business find his or her experience exceeding expectations. They invest more in your products and services and they sing your praises to anyone in need of similar products and services.

If Mrs. Jones at the sandwich shop in our example tells one of her friends how fresh the vegetables are because she's been invited to test them out, and if her friends know how picky she can be, then they may well be inspired to try the shop out for themselves.

WOW Moments have many positive sides to them. They can turn an average day into a special day for one of your customers. They can give a personal boost to the person who created the moment. But make no mistake that they also shine a positive light on your business, increase customer loyalty, and generate more revenue down the road.

Attitude is a dominant player in every aspect of our lives. Perhaps that goes without saying, but the fact that we are in charge of our attitude means that we can also influence the attitude of others, either positively or negatively.

Your customers are actually asking you to influence their attitude. Some are actually challenging you to do so. If you're in business, this is a challenge you have to be willing to accept. In fact, it should be a challenge you cherish. The reason is simple. People whose attitude you influence in a positive way are likely to be better customers. They might not spend more money at your sandwich shop when they come in, but they will likely return. Of course, you have to provide them with a good product; in this case a great sandwich. And if you want to create a WOW Moment in the process, throw in a fresh cookie for free or a coupon for $2.00 off the next time they come in.

The WOW Moment concept is all about influencing the attitudes of your customers in a positive way and creating an emotional attachment to your business, product, or service. And when you and your staff approach the concept with a positive attitude, you're halfway there.

CHAPTER TWENTY-ONE

WOW Moments and the Power of Emotional Engagement

As a leader, you know what it means to talk about vision. Vision is the dream. Big or small, it doesn't matter. A vision may be long term or it may deal with an immediate issue or opportunity.

Another leader within Humana whom I admire greatly is Peter Edwards. Peter is a visionary. He is someone who truly embodies the principles of the WOW Moment from a leadership perspective and has an uncanny ability to bring out the best in his team. I often catch myself saying things in meetings that I unknowingly have borrowed from him. For instance, when I'm meeting with my team, and we start talking about a matter out in the future, I'll often say, 'Well, you know what, if I could dream about it..." – whatever *it* is – "...it would be this."

I might say something as simple as: "It would be a situation where no patient would ever have to worry about a referral. He or she would be in the exam room with the doctor, the doctor would have the means to process every bit of information at his fingertips, and all that information would intuitively get around to the referral coordinator. The referral coordinator would coordinate the patient's next appointments on the spot. The patient would leave the examination room feeling well taken care of. She would walk to the checkout counter, and it would be all done, right down to her prescriptions waiting for her there. That's my dream."

Okay, it sounds simple on the one hand: a no-hassle referral system. But to me, that's vision.

Vision is a place to get to, a situation to aspire to, a goal to pursue. It is what you are striving for.

Your vision sets the tone for an entire team. It fuels the strategy and tactics that everyone down the line will be implementing in his quest to realize that vision.

The WOW Moment concept is a tool that gives color and impetus to a company's visions. WOW Moments add value to the products and services that you provide your clients or your customers (in our case, our patients).

Whatever your industry is, you want the members of your team to rise above the service basics that form the foundation of your customer experience. WOW Moments are the perfect vehicle for doing this.

Everyone in your industry has a service basic; it might not be exactly the same as yours, but it does exist. If all you ask of your team is to meet the service basic, then you're pretty much like everyone else. That might be okay if you don't care about customer loyalty and creating an environment where your customers are out there stirring up business for you.

Make no mistake, customers in every industry, big and small, want more than the service basic, they want special treatment.

They want to be treated as if they matter to you and your team. Yes, they want their expectations met, but what they really want is for the people they do business with to exceed those expectations. It doesn't matter if you run a car wash or a car dealership, a pharmacy or a hardware store, a mutual fund or an insurance company, customers want to deal with someone who cares that they are about to put down their hard-earned money for a product or service. Creating WOW Moments is the best way I know to show your customers that they are special, that they are worth some extra effort.

Let's take the pharmacy we mentioned above. Their service basic includes common courtesy and dispensing accurate prescriptions in a timely fashion. These days they have to ask customers if they need or want information or instructions regarding their prescriptions. The problem is, every pharmacy in the country is pretty much the same from a service basic perspective. How can one pharmacy separate itself from another? They almost all have automated phone service; plug in your prescription number and a computer passes the information on. But what about a courtesy call informing you that your prescription is ready or a free mobile app that did the same thing? What about a real voice delivering the message? What about a real person calling you to say you might have a problem with your insurance instead of waiting for you to show up so he can deliver the bad news? Now we're getting to a WOW Moment. And when you arrive to pick up your prescription, what if the pharmacist himself came over and said thanks for coming in? What if you were able to use a drive-through instead of parking your car and going inside? How about free delivery?

The question a WOW Moment advocate always asks is: what is the customer expecting? When you have an answer to that question, you can visualize exceeding that expectation and moving the experience to something extraordinary.

At that point you've left the service basic in the dust, and you've left your competition in the dust as well.

In the healthcare industry, we face a most interesting and disturbing dilemma. Patients have come to expect poor service in healthcare. And not only expect it, but accept it. For example, how often are we as patients asked to wait upwards of an hour, and sometimes much more, for an appointment to see the doctor? The appointment is at one in the afternoon. We show up on time. We're expected to show up on time. We sign in. We take a seat in the waiting room. We have time to read an entire magazine, one that's two months old but all they have.

Amazingly, no one seems to question this; we just accept it. We may not like it, but we accept it. I often ask myself if this suggests that we as a society have come to expect and accept poor customer service? Is it a general state of mind, or one that is seemingly accepted only in healthcare?

The point is that most of us are ripe for WOW Moments. Something that takes what we expect as customers – which sometimes isn't that much – and really sends a powerful message that we are important. That opens up a lot of blue sky for your business, because taking the customer experience and climbing the stairway of surprise is something we can all do. It's not science or research or innovation as much as it is relationship building, as much as it is creating a bond.

WOW Moments are about emotional engagement when all is said and done.

Even the associate who introduced fruit cups to our waiting room regimen was tapping into the emotions of our patients.

Here is a different kind of example, but one that paints in broad strokes how big a part emotional engagement plays in changing the culture of your enterprise in a positive way.

In the 1990s, American Express changed its leadership at the top, hiring Ken Chenault as its new CEO, and he in turn took this powerhouse company down a completely new path with regard to emotional engagement. This was back in a time when credit card companies were dumping clients and/or charging fees that made little sense. Not AMEX. Under Chenault's tutelage, they decided to focus more on creating experiences and differentiating their cards with the belief that customers would pay additional money if they thought they were being treated differently and if they felt the company was trying to create a closer relationship with them. Enter the American Express Platinum and Black cards. No, these cards weren't for everyone. They were for a unique brand of customer, a special, even elite, brand of customer. At least that was the image the company was creating. And along with the image came the ability to charge annual fees of $500 and $1,500 respectively. People bought in. They felt as if AMEX was elevating their customer experience. And with that came record profits and a reputation for being the most sought after cards in the world.

AMEX created a bond with its clients and created emotional engagement.

Pulling the Platinum or Black card out of your wallet was like a recurring WOW Moment. You felt special. You felt powerful.

When you solve the problem of creating a WOW Moment for customers, when you find exactly the right device to elevate their customer experience and blow their expectations right out of the water, you create this emotionally charged bond. And once done, it is nearly impossible for anyone else to replicate.

Before I moved from my house in Sunny Isles Beach, I had a favorite Starbucks. My favorite Starbucks had my favorite barista: Shirley. Shirley knew my name. She knew my drink. She knew exactly how I liked it. She knew what scone I preferred. She knew how much I liked her smile and her greeting. It got to a point where my espresso macchiato and pumpkin scone were already in the pipeline by the time I got through the line and to the counter, all thanks to someone who understood the WOW Moment concept, even if she didn't have a name for it.

Then I moved. I know the Starbucks down the block from my new place will have the same espresso macchiato and the same pumpkin scone, but they don't have Shirley and the WOW Moment that Shirley provided me every morning. Now my new Starbucks may have a barista with the same ability and the same willingness to provide me with a WOW Moment, and I'm hoping that's true. But my expectations have changed. I want Shirley, but now I have to dial down my expectation and hope the service basic at my new haunt will be at least as good as at the old place. Who knows, it might actually be better. At the moment, I doubt it. And it is that doubt that makes me ripe for another WOW Moment created by another caring barista.

———

It is this emotion of doubt that leaves me open to the kind of unexpected engagement that all customers are just waiting for.

———

For me, part of my leadership role is to demonstrate a willingness to build emotional engagement. You can't preach it. You can't say, "While I'm sitting here behind my desk, I want you all to go out there and foster emotional engagement with our clients." Won't work. You have to show it. You have to lead by example.

―――

This emotional engagement comes naturally to some people; that is a great start in implementing the WOW Moment concept.

―――

In others, it is teachable. The best way to teach it is to demonstrate it yourself, show someone a WOW Moment. It's not just for your customers; WOW Moments are for everyone. If you want loyal employees, create a WOW Moment. Bring them lunch. Give them a pat on the back. Send them a gift card. Tell them how much you appreciate their efforts. And then listen for them to say, "Wow, I didn't expect that."

Don't get me wrong. Not everyone is inherently able to create a WOW Moment on behalf of your company. Not everyone is inherently able to create a WOW Moment with her spouse, children, best friend, or worst enemy. She either can't understand the concept or chooses not to embrace it. No problem.

You have to make the WOW Moment concept part of your training. Most people will be struck by the power of the message, because they can imagine what a WOW Moment feels like. They can imagine making an experience extraordinary; they can imagine it happening to them. And, they can imagine how good it feels. Training your employees to understand and embrace a new company culture is essential. You can't send out a memo. You have to demonstrate the concept; you have to exemplify the concept. You have to make it a part of your company's value system. The concept can't be a choice. You have to be willing to say, "We are going to embrace the WOW Moment concept as a part of our daily interaction with customers and with each other."

Then you start to hire the right kind of people, people with a WOW Moment mentality, people who understand emotional engagement or at the very least can be trained to understand.

CHAPTER TWENTY-TWO

The Personal Connection

WOW Moments are not reserved for the workplace any more than they are for the home or the community. Any experience can be made extraordinary by introducing the WOW Moment concept, and any interaction can be made even more special.

All relationships begin with certain basics. Being courteous. Being honest. Being genuine. Even the most casual relationship has to be founded in these three elements or it cannot truly be called a relationship.

Any "meaningful" relationship, however, calls for something beyond these basics. All meaningful relationships begin when we make a true connection. There is an emotional component to a true connection. If you care about making someone's day a bit better, with a kind word or a kind gesture, then you've added an emotional component.

This element of caring – on whatever level that might be – is essential to the WOW Moment concept.

Sometimes it's just a matter of paying attention. What does your spouse really want? Just to know that you're paying attention; that you're aware of her needs; that you care about what she's thinking and what she's interested in. You can't have a WOW Moment if you're not paying attention, because you won't see the opportunity when it presents itself.

One man told me that the most important thing he did when planning his wife's birthday outing was to leave his cell phone at home. This was a WOW Moment for her. It said, "I'm paying attention to you and only you tonight." It may sound ridiculously simplistic, but it worked for this couple simply because he never left his cell phone at home.

Similarly, a woman told me that she celebrated her husband's fortieth birthday by planning a hike in the mountains. This was a WOW Moment for her husband, because it was so out of character for her; she was not the outdoors type. But this woman was paying attention. She understood how much the outdoors meant to her husband, and she realized she had not been participating in his love of nature. She went out of her comfort zone and far exceeded his birthday expectations in doing so.

If paying attention is the first essential in creating a true connection, then authenticity is the second.

I call it "authentically in the moment." You and I can understand the WOW Moment concept. We can visualize exceeding someone's expectation, be it a customer, a spouse, or the man on the street. We can intelligently discuss taking the customer experience or the spousal experience and making it extraordinary. But when the time comes to leave that cell phone at home when you're going out to dinner or going for that hike on your husband's birthday, there has to be authenticity attached to the act. Otherwise the recipient will see through the moment in a heartbeat and the only "wow" we'll produce will be in response to our disingenuousness.

A WOW Moment that backfires due to a lack of sincerity is far worse than no WOW Moment at all.

———

The last component in making a true connection is a focus on the overall experience.

———

The man who leaves his cell phone at home with the intent of wowing his spouse at dinner, and then forgets to make the dinner reservation and picks her up late, just blew the whole thing. The woman who plans a hike for her husband's birthday and then shows up for the hike wearing high-heeled shoes doesn't demonstrate either authenticity or a focus on the overall experience.

Look back on an earlier example where the associate at one of our medical centers began supplying our patients with fruit cups in the waiting room; she would not have made the splash she made had the fruit not been fresh. This would have shown a lack of focus on the details of the overall experience. In fact, this WOW Moment experience is a great example of grasping the overall experience and creating something extraordinary.

This fine and important melding of paying attention to detail, authenticity, and a focus on the overall experience is not as easy as it seems. After I left college, a friend and I started an IT recruiting company called Network Connections Group; I described the nature of the business back in Chapter Two. Our focus was on the IT industry. Joe was an IT specialist, and I was in charge of making connections and networking. For two young guys we made pretty good money, enough that I could buy myself a very nice car, and buying myself a very nice car had, I admit, been a dream of mine in my twenties.

So I went shopping. I admit up front that I was young and probably looked even younger. First stop: the local Mercedes dealership; yes, I was feeling my oats. I looked around the car lot and then went into the showroom. Three salesmen glanced over. Not one of them said hello or came over to offer his assistance. I left and went to a local BMW dealership. Same scenario. A few people looked my way, but no one approached me; it was very apparent that they didn't see me as a legitimate prospect. I remember that there was an older couple browsing at the same time. One of the BMW salesmen walked right past me, said not a word, and fell into conversation with this older couple. I could almost hear him thinking: "This kid can't afford one of our cars, so I'm going to focus on a couple who can." No WOW Moments here.

I actually sat in several cars and kicked a couple of tires. I know I looked interested, but all these guys could see was my youth. They didn't see a youthful customer. They saw a kid messing around in their showroom. A terrible way to do business.

Same scenario later that morning at a local Ford dealership. Not one salesman engaged me in conversation. Not one salesman tried to explore my needs or educate me about their cars. They broke all three rules of a true connection: paying attention, authenticity, and focusing on the overall experience.

So I left. I drove three blocks to the local Acura dealership. I had done my research and was interested in looking at the Acura TL.

The moment I walked in and circled the TL, a nicely dressed salesman came up to me and said, "Ah! I notice you're looking at the TL. Do you know what this car can do?"

This was an interesting approach. He didn't ask me if I needed help. He didn't ask me if I was old enough to drive. He didn't look at me like I was out of place in his showroom. He took a different tack, and one I found engaging: *I see you're looking at the TL. Do you know what this car can do?*

In response I said, "No, I haven't a clue what this car can do."

"Let me show you." Not pushy. Not rude. Genuine.

Perfect; he had me. We went through all the different features of the car, and I was amazed. He asked a series of questions around what I liked to do, what I wanted in a car, and what my expectations were. We took a test drive; it drove even better than I expected. We talked price. The TL was essentially the same price as the BMW I was looking at earlier and slightly less than the Mercedes I never got a chance to test drive.

At the end of the day, I bought the Acura. I paid cash.

―――

The salesman satisfied our three criteria: he paid attention; he was authentic; he focused on the overall experience. And he made a sale.

―――

To this day, I am still amazed at the failure of the other three car dealerships to satisfy even one of these criteria. They failed equally at fulfilling any of the elements of a service basic. They didn't even say hello. If I were the owner of those dealerships, I'd be telling my sales staff in no uncertain terms: "You acknowledge every person who comes through the door. You say hello to everyone. It doesn't matter if they are six years old, 46, or 76. It doesn't matter if they have gold and diamonds flowing off of them or are wearing ripped jeans. You acknowledge everyone. If you notice them looking at a particular car, you ask how you can assist them in the process."

Those are the most rudimentary elements of a service basic, and those three dealerships met none of them. The salesman at the Acura dealership started with the service basic, but immediately elevated the customer experience with his approach and his attitude. He treated me like the only customer in the world, and that WOW Moment turned into a sale.

The moral of the story is that you can't get to the experience if you fail at the basics.

A genuine greeting seems too obvious even to mention, but every service basic begins there. You can't have a true connection if you don't start at the beginning. You might think: "Well, you don't have to teach an employee how to greet someone when he comes in the door."

At CAC, we don't take that chance. We actually go so far as to train our employees using scripted greetings, and we practice them until they become second nature. This is even truer in a day and age when electronic communication makes it so easy for people to ignore the formalities of proper etiquette.

If you're in business, you want your customers to know why your company and your people are different from the competition. You want them to recognize the superior quality of your products and services. And you don't want them to have to dig for it like a needle in a haystack.

At CAC, we're pretty bold about this.

When a patient or potential patients come into one of our centers, we don't mince words. After an appropriate greeting, we say, in effect, "Let us give you a brief tour and show you why we are different."

We show them our wellness center where a group of seniors might be doing exercises. We show them our activity center where the family of a patient might be playing Wii or a group of patients might be playing dominos or bingo. We show them the physician moving from patient to patient with his or her care team.

We walk them over and show them where they can get their eye exam and eyeglasses right on site. We show them our on-site pharmacy. We talk about the 13 different specialties represented right here in our center. We talk about expediting services. We talk about personalized care. We do everything we can to elevate the experience, because we know we're not the only healthcare facility in South Florida. We do everything we can to create a personalized connection the minute someone walks in the door, because we know that is at the heart of every WOW Moment.

CHAPTER TWENTY-THREE

Customers for Life

We talked earlier in the book about the concept of *La Familia,* that sense of family, community, and continuity where your approach to the customer experience is such that every person who walks through door – even if the "door" happens to be off-site or online – feels a sense of place in your establishment or a tie to your company based upon something special.

In the previous chapter, I told you the story about the Acura dealership and the WOW Moment that led to the purchase of a new car. It turned out that the dealership (Rick Case Acura) was owned by a husband and wife team. They personally sent me a postcard of thanks after my purchase and invited me to a year-end holiday party where patrons contributed gifts for needy children in the area. They wanted more than a one-time customer. They wanted to create a relationship, a sense of family. Now if you can do that in the car industry, you can do it in pretty much any industry.

WOW Moments and *La Familia* go hand in hand; the WOW Moment elevates the experience, an exceptional experience leads to a true connection, and true connections are at the heart of any family.

What is the end game of all this talk about *La Familia*, true connections, and WOW Moments? The end game is customer retention. Building a relationship with every customer that keeps him coming back for more. Yes, you have to start with an excellent product or exceptional services. You can't fake that. No quantity of WOW Moments can overcome a poor product or ineffective service. No debate there. But all things being equal in that regard, elevating the customer experience is the surest way to retain that customer you spent so much time cultivating in the first place.

Most industries are extremely competitive. We touched on the car business last chapter; do you know how many car dealerships there are in South Florida? A lot. And they are all competing for your business. Even dealerships that sell the same brand are competing with each other.

The element I love most about the healthcare industry, and the thing that motivates me the most, is the many services we can offer to our community.

I love the fact that we can make a palpable difference in people's lives. It is, nonetheless, extremely competitive. There are lots of places where Floridians can seek medical attention. I cherish the competition. The competition is what drives us to work harder, work smarter, and work more efficiently. The competition is what makes us want to elevate the customer experience to something exceptional. The competition is what drives innovation. And the competition is what drove me to develop the WOW Moment concept.

Much like your business I'm sure, at CAC we wake up with the goal of making our healthcare products and services the best they can be. Best doctors, best nurses, best associates, best facilities. We may not be able to control the advancement of technology in our industry, but we can do our best to provide our patients with the latest and the greatest.

If you're in the car business, you can't control the design or manufacture of the new year models, but you can know everything there is to know about these new vehicles, what makes them different from those offered by the dealership down the street, and what they offer the customer that makes them special.

So whether you are selling healthcare or Hondas, what you can control is the customer experience.

What all customers want is to feel as if they are valued as a customer, even if they're just looking around, and that their business is valued. If there is that sense of caring that comes with *La Familia*, there is not a customer, client, or patient alive who won't respond positively and likely give you their business for as long as that feeling exists.

If you can enlist someone as a customer for life, rest assured it's because you elevated his experience to the extraordinary. And you can be pretty sure there were some very special WOW Moments involved along the way.

I know this much: if one of your customers, clients, or patients has experienced a WOW Moment, you've got him. You've got the bond I've been describing. You've done it. It is a bond that keeps giving.

I love to use teachers as examples when I'm talking about WOW Moments. Teachers do one thing: they serve. They serve their students. They serve parents. They serve the educational community.

My own son is a great example. Corey has his own learning style. He has a way of processing that isn't completely linear; in fact, he sometimes begins at the end and works backward. This was, for a long time, a problem for Corey in the traditional school setting, and no one really identified it for quite some time. One his teachers, however, took a particular interest. Corey was in sixth grade at the time, and I remember Mrs. Fuller saying to me, "Your son is very smart, but there is something going on processing-wise that is making it hard for him to keep up. And he has a tendency to rush things, and that doesn't help matters."

Mrs. Fuller's concern and her observations prompted us to do some testing. Some people recommended medication. I didn't want to do that. Nor did Corey's teacher. We wanted to maximize his strengths, not mask his weaknesses. We started an outside teaching module that my son immediately took to. But what helped as much as anything were the afterhours, one-on-one teaching and counseling sessions that Mrs. Fuller provided to him. Mrs. Fuller did it because she saw Corey's potential. She did it because she cared. And the results were awesome. But the thing that stands out about this wonderful interaction – the WOW Moment, if you will – was her willingness to go above and beyond. I know there are lots of teachers who say, "This is my job. I am just here to open a book. I am just here to provide the basics." They have a service basic mentality, and that guides their actions.

I can hear them saying, "My service basic is this. I am going to educate these children. I am going to have a lesson plan. I am going to ensure that they understand the lesson plan. I am going to work with them to ensure that they understand the course and the material, I know that a certain percentage of them won't pass or understand the course material, and that's understood."

Not this teacher. Mrs. Fuller was dedicated to the overall educational experience. She loved her job. It was a calling. She wasn't satisfied with the percentages. When she saw a learning style that didn't fit the mold, she went out of her way to maximize that learning style. She wanted every student to succeed.

Teaching was a series of WOW Moments to this woman; going above and beyond was the norm, not the exception.

Corey graduated from high school with honors and as vice president of his class. And although he is in college now, he remembers Mrs. Fuller to this day. So do I.

There is a further lesson to be learned here. While our goal in business may be the long-term retention of our customers, clients, or patients, making a difference right now, in this moment, is what the WOW Moment concept is truly about. And while we can acknowledge that making the customer experience extraordinary can likely have long-term ramifications, WOW Moments are essentially present tense. Right now. How can I make your experience better today, whether it's bringing your car in for a tune-up at the local garage, making the referral process at the medical center easier and more streamlined, or making a kid feel special about his progress in class.

Yes, your long-term goal is a customer for life, but like most things, it begins with small steps: knowing what the service basic is and going beyond it; knowing a client's expectations and exceeding them; understanding the WOW Moments concept and creating them one at a time.

Let's use the restaurant business as an example. A great restaurant is about the quality of the food, sure, but it's also about the people who own the restaurant and the people who work there. How much they enjoy what they're doing. The positive energy they emit. How happy they are to see you come in the door. The conversation the waitperson makes with you.

If the chef comes out and asks how your meal was, that's elevating the experience. If the manager buys your table a round of drinks, that's probably above and beyond your expectations. It's a moment-by-moment experience that the people at the restaurant hope brings you back again and again and establishes that customer for life we're talking about.

One of my favorite stories is about the guy and his wife who go to Las Vegas for a couple of shows and a night or two away from the kids. His wife loves the cooking shows on the Food Channel, and one of her favorite chefs happens to own a restaurant in Caesar's Palace. Of course, she has to experience it.

When they arrive, the place is overflowing with people and they fight their way through the crowd. The waiter, on the other hand, is calm and friendly. He indulges the guy's wife in a story about the restaurant's world-famous owner and recommends the Pork Tenderloin, one of their specialties. It's sensational. The waiter even spends a few moments telling the wife about the dish's special ingredients. She kiddingly asks for the recipe.

When their meal is over, a man comes up to the table and hands her a neatly printed page with the recipe on it. And guess what? It's the world-famous restaurant owner himself. He actually spends two minutes walking the guy's wife through the recipe and giving her hints about the preparation. He shakes their hands, says, "Thanks for coming in," and is gone. That's a WOW Moment. And will the man and his wife come back the next time they're in Vegas? Guaranteed.

The truth is, in most businesses, you spend a good deal of your energy in the short term, trying to make sure the day-to-day customer experience is exceptional.

Every well-run business has long-term goals and a strategy to reach those goals. Those goals and that strategy are essential, and your team should be aware of them. But it is the tactical side that drives the strategy, and the tactical side includes the service basics, the small things we do to understand a customer's expectations and to exceed them, and the WOW Moments we create.

The WOW Moment culture that we're building at my medical centers is long term in nature; it's a strategy that I see as elevating us above our competition and developing customers for life. But WOW Moments themselves – like the manager of our restaurant buying us a round of drinks, for example – are tactical. They are short-term acts that we hope create customer loyalty down the road.

CHAPTER TWENTY-FOUR

Acquisition, Growth, and the WOW Moment Culture

You're in business. You deem your business a success. Like we have done at CAC with the WOW Moment concept, you have developed a culture that serves your business well and gives you a sense of pride and accomplishment.

You have three choices. You can maintain the status quo, you can expand, or you can acquire.

The status quo is not always such a bad thing. You may say, "We've got a good thing going, and I'm not going to mess with it." Here's an example. There is a jazz club in Miami that I often frequent. It's small, cramped, and wildly successful. The place draws the best musicians and is always crowded. One night I asked the owner, "Why don't you expand into the space next door? Double your size?" His answer: "I've got a great thing going here. People know exactly what to expect when they come in. So do the musicians. I'm not messing with a good thing." Okay, I get it.

Choice two: you expand. You open a new location. You add to your product line. You add a new service or two. You invest in what you currently have.

Choice three: you grow via acquisition. You buy up your competition.

———

In CAC's case, we've both expanded and acquired. But we have done both while preserving at all costs the culture that makes it all possible.

———

We have scouted new locations and built new facilities, taking with us all the things that make us successful at our current locations, including the culture we've been embracing for years now, a culture that places its emphasis on our medical centers, our services, and, most importantly, our end user – the patient. Since I became the company's CEO, we have expanded into five new facilities. So far, all have performed at or better than expected economically, and the WOW Moment culture has been soundly endorsed.

We have also been cautiously aggressive in acquiring other medical facilities. To date, we have acquired six facilities around the state of Florida. In doing so, I have created what I call acquisition spheres: **Economic + Strategic + Cultural.**

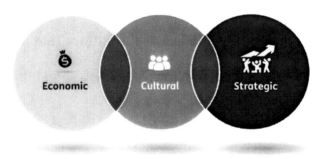

There are three distinct areas that play into the extensive due diligence that we perform throughout the process: the economic, the strategic, and the cultural.

Of course, the economics are critical; we have no intention of acquiring a medical center that does not have the potential to be successful from a financial standpoint. As you would if you were acquiring a new asset, we look at everything from the quality of the facilities to the demographics of the potential customer base. We consider the strategic aspects of the business and its geography. Does it provide a barrier to entry or allow us to go on the offensive? Where is it? What are the population and growth patterns affecting the area?

And lastly, and most germane to our discussions here, we study the current culture of the target organization. The question is more straightforward than you might think, and you'll have to ask the same one whether you own a car dealership, a yoga studio, or an investment firm. That is: Does the culture of the target organization really meld into your organization? If the answer is not exactly, then are there synergies that can nonetheless make the marriage viable? I can't tell you how critical this is to the WOW Moment way of thinking.

I've seen organizations fall apart because they don't take the time to assess the culture of their intended target. Do they align with the culture you've worked so hard to establish? I've also seen organizations fall apart because they didn't take the time to integrate their culture into their new acquisition (or acquisitions) to ensure the necessary synergies required for long-term success. So, they instead manage two completely separate assets and waste money by having duplicative resources utilized.

CAC is a good example. Now that we have instituted the WOW Moment culture throughout our organization, we want to adapt it without exception as we move forward in our growth. That being said, we always look for acquisitions that, at the very least, demonstrate the potential to acclimate to the WOW Moment culture.

To begin, we want to see a medical center that, at the very least, is delivering on the service basics that we have been discussing throughout this book. Without this, there is no basis for understanding and maximizing the customer experience.

The assessment of the service basics is a hands-on process. We visit the center anonymously. We see how people are greeted. We look for positive and genuine interaction. We judge the atmosphere in the facility. We see if there is an emphasis on the end user and her needs. You might say, "But these things can be taught.

This attitude can be learned." Yes, but there are limits. Realistically, you begin by asking if there are the resources available for such a massive cultural shift. I have learned not to underestimate this undertaking. Negative cultures, like negative behaviors, are not easy to amend. If you can't meet the service basics, you can't understand a patient experience, which means you can never elevate that experience to the extraordinary.

This cultural exploration, if you will, usually gets serious once we've taken a hard look at a potential target's economic potential and financial health. Once there is a feeling that the economics make sense, then we press ahead with our cultural appraisal. We have stages in the due diligence. We survey the organization's leadership; we call this Due Diligence 1. The bottom line of this anonymous survey is to assess how the organization's leaders lead. How do they define purpose? How do they motivate? How do they meld strategy and tactics?

Due Diligence 2 takes it down to the rank and file. We want to know how people are incentivized within the organization; how promotions are granted within the organization; how people are recognized for their achievements and contributions within the organization. Are rewards and incentives linked with the patient experience; are the employees satisfied with their working environment; are their expectations as employees being met? Lastly, what would they like to see being done differently, if anything?

We stress the recognition piece because the way an organization recognizes the accomplishments and achievements of its employees and staff tells you a lot about its culture.

Does a company understand the employee experience? Does a company take the time to understand and respect the expectations and hopes of its employees? Does the organization use the job to hold its employees hostage, or does it try to give its employees a sense of ownership with regard to the company? Does an organization have any sense of the WOW Moment concept when it comes to its people? Does it see a job as a calling or as just a job with a paycheck attached? Is work fun? Is there a sense of camaraderie?

If the CEO of a company takes the time to recognize the achievements of his or her staff by sending a handwritten note or visiting the factory floor, that tells me that the culture favors the end user. It's not about corporate; it's about the people on the firing line, the men and women dealing with customers and clients and representing the organization at the grassroots level. That's what I'm looking for in a company culture.

Over time, a well-established culture becomes ingrained in the psyches of an organization's men and women.

A company's culture affects its employees' outlook on their jobs and the people they come in contact with every day. It affects their behavior. If the culture is one that focuses on the bottom line at all costs, then this short-term attitude influences everyone and everything. If the culture is one that emphasizes customer service and customer relations, then this long-term approach allows for a focus on the customer experience. If you think a change of ownership in and of itself can immediately turn an unhealthy culture on its head, you may be right, but just don't expect overnight miracles.

The one thing I discovered when I took the reins at CAC is that the institution of a culture that fully respects the rank and file, celebrates their contributions relative to the company's goals, and gives them a sense of ownership is a lot easier to sell than one which puts the bottom line first.

So while I will jump more readily at the acquisition of a medical center that emphasizes the service basic, and understands the customer experience and its importance to the success of the company, I won't necessarily shy away from acquiring a group with a negative culture. I have seen how readily people embrace the WOW Moment culture that puts the end user first, that turns the spotlight away from the corporate level, and that places the spotlight on the men and women who serve our patients.

I always asked this when accessing a target acquisition: "How much work is it going to take to institute the WOW Moment culture, and can we really overcome the problems created by the negative culture currently bringing the target down?"

You can't have two cultures and be sustainable. Acquisitions must fit within your organization's cultural vision.

From the C-Suite to the front line, everyone will have to buy in to the new culture you're establishing or it won't work. At the end of the day, this is about growing as a company. If there are going to be forces within the newly acquired entity that serve to impede this goal, then you have to decide whether the acquisition is worth it. Can employees be effectively retrained? Can management be won over? If you've embraced the WOW Moment concept, then you've made a promise to your customers that elevating their experience is your top priority. Any new acquisition has to embrace this philosophy. If wholesale changes need to be made, so be it. However, you will have to decide if making such changes is commercially viable. Do you have enough resources (time and money) to do the job effectively and without damaging the reputation your organization has established elsewhere? Whether you're growing internally or growing via acquisition, there has to be a balance between the economic ramifications and the cultural implications.

I will never sacrifice the culture that we've worked so hard to build at CAC, because I know how much the WOW Moment concept has contributed to our success.

I always weigh the cultural, economic, and strategic spheres equally. They have to mesh. When they do, you're probably onto something special. When they don't, you have to have the smarts, courage, and good sense to look elsewhere.

CHAPTER TWENTY-FIVE

The WOW Moment Culture

WOW Moments are not about making a sale.

WOW Moments are not about enticing your customer, client, or patient into spending more on your products or services.

WOW Moments are not about stealing a customer away from a competitor.

Yes, all of these things may well happen in the course of your interaction with that customer, client, or patient – all positive results – but those results are only one of the many reasons for promoting the WOW Moment culture.

―――

WOW Moments are about understanding the customer experience and doing something to take it to the next level, what we have been calling the "extraordinary."

―――

WOW Moments are about understanding a customer's expectations and doing everything we can to exceed them.

WOW Moments are about moving customers to a place where they want to share their experience with friends, family, and associates, effectively becoming a partner in promoting your business, in our case at CAC, a net promoter for our medical centers, our people, and our services.

WOW Moments are about creating an environment in which customer retention is a given, where a customer says, "I wouldn't go anywhere else."

WOW Moments are about building long-term relationships, about showing how much you care moment by moment, and about allowing your customers to see who you really are as an organization.

As I have said throughout this book, a Wow Moment can take any experience, personal or professional, and make it extraordinary. A Wow Moment takes what we expect from a situation or interaction and elevates it to the unexpected: the nurse who brings a rose into a patient's room every morning, the teacher who goes into the community and meets with parents at the local recreation center, the CEO who calls one supplier or customer every day just to say thanks.

We've talked mostly about creating Wow Moments that elevate the stature of your business in your customer's eyes, but I want to emphasize how Wow Moments can infuse meaning and wonder into personal relationships. A man shows up at his wife's workplace with a dozen roses; a son or daughter surprises his or her parents with an all-inclusive vacation to Cancun; a group of co-workers gets together to help the business next door with flood damage caused by a broken pipe.

WOW Moments, as we have discovered, come in all shapes and sizes. Some are inspiring. Some are life changing. Some just make for a better day. All are about people.

———

Everything we do as human beings is really about our search for relationships and connections.

———

We may be solitary beings from a physical standpoint, but it is in our nature to build bridges.

One thing I have discovered is that building bridges starts with a foundation of caring. For you, this might come naturally. For your partner, it might have to be learned and cultivated. In any case, this foundation of caring just naturally leads to more positive interactions. All of a sudden, we're taking action and solving problems. All of a sudden, our relationships are becoming more important and more meaningful. All of a sudden, we want to be better human beings and to offer something above and beyond the average experience.

Exceptional interactions are at the heart of the WOW Moment concept because the vast majority come from a foundation of service.

We talked earlier about helping a client or customer identify and define how he views a successful relationship or a successful business transaction; a WOW Moment is essentially the art of providing something above and beyond this definition. You pull into a car wash with certain expectations, and the attendant runs your car through a second time because he sees a few spots they've missed; your favorite restaurant surprises you with a 40% off coupon to celebrate your birthday; the line manager in a factory shows up with boxes of Girl Scout cookies for her entire crew.

Connecting in a positive way – even if it's as simple as the examples mentioned above – gives you credibility; it gives you credibility not only in the eyes of your customers and your clients, but also in the eyes of your superiors, your peers, and your teams.

We all have a series of filters when we're dealing with other people, particularly in the workplace. These filters allow us to make decisions about another person's character, motives, and authenticity. If our filters identify a person who is unresponsive or lacks caring, our first instinct is to move on and move on quickly. A natural part of building relationships is to test the other person's sincerity. Bona fide connections are built upon honesty and authenticity, and a lack of sincerity is pretty easy to unmask.

You can't generate a WOW Moment if you're insincere, or less than honest, or lacking in authenticity. It just doesn't work.

Genuine connections come from a place of caring and concern, and so do WOW Moments. You have to mean them.

How many times have you seen another person drop his guard because some instinct tells him that he is dealing with someone who is genuine and genuinely cares? It's human nature. This is when that someone tells you what success looks like in his eyes. And more importantly, he also tells you where the "WOW" is for him. Creating a WOW Moment is easy at that point. For some patients in our medical centers, a nurse engaging them in conversation about their grandkids is unexpected and appreciated; they relax, they feel welcome; they think, "Wow, that was so nice of her."

And as we talked about earlier, there is added benefit for the nurse in this situation as well, because WOW Moments add value to the job; there is a sense of self-worth that comes from creating these special moments.

I have learned over the years that showing your true self and allowing yourself to be vulnerable are at the heart of a true connection, and fundamental to creating WOW Moments.

You and I have to be willing to give of ourselves. Conversely, we also have to be willing to receive. Giving and receiving are action statements, and taking action can be scary. So yes, creating a WOW Moment can sometimes be a bit scary; you don't know how it's going to be received, so you're putting yourself on the line. However, I can say with absolute certainty that WOW Moments are rarely, if ever, refused. Why? Because people want to connect! It is human nature to want a relationship built around trust and self-honesty, and that's at the center of the WOW Moment culture. So is going beyond the expected, whether we're talking about the workplace or the home front, family, friends, or neighbors.

If it's expected, then it's not a WOW.

We said this back in Chapter One: most personal connections are emotionally based. We also said that our emotions and our behaviors cannot be separated, because our behaviors are predicated, most often, upon an emotional reaction.

WOW Moments send a positive message to the brain. They also send a positive message to the heart. That's why they feel so good.

From a purely business point of view, I can tell you that customers, clients, and patients remember WOW Moments because they trigger positive reactions from both the head and the heart. And if that makes for good business, it's safe to say that it also makes for a good marriage, a terrific friendship, or a potentially meaningful acquaintance.

It's a two-way street. If you go the extra mile to elevate an experience or to exceed someone's expectation, if you go out of your way to create a WOW Moment, it will be just as rewarding for you as it is for the person on the other end. That's pretty cool.

Let's say a friend of yours is moving, and you show up unexpectedly to help. And you even bring coffee. That's a WOW Moment. Let's say one of our associates shows up an hour early for work so that she can take one of our patients out to the rose garden before her chemotherapy session. That's a WOW Moment. Let's say you leave a bouquet of flowers and a handwritten thank you note for the women who clean your office every night. That's a WOW Moment.

In the workplace, the WOW Moment culture begins with a service mentality at the foundation. If the people in your organization know that their focus, first and foremost, has to be on service, it becomes an expectation. This expectation then passes naturally down to your customers. That's a great start. Now you have a baseline that you try to exceed with every interaction. Now we're getting closer to the WOW Moment culture.

You set your standards high throughout your organization, and then you grow from there.

Unless you're in a completely automated industry, the WOW Moment concept is applicable. Let's break it down. Where there are humans involved, there is human interaction: communication, commitment, hope, fear, love, tolerance, success, failure. Where there is this amazing breadth of interaction there are connections, some deep, some less so. Where there are connections at any level, there are expectations. With expectations comes the opportunity to step up your game and go beyond what is expected in that interaction. That's when you begin creating experience. That's when you open the door to a WOW Moment.

It doesn't matter what industry you're in – whether you're manufacturing cars, building bridges, or running a hospital – and it doesn't matter the size of your company – whether you have a thousand employees or none – the WOW Moment concept is always based upon the end user.

Big or small, service oriented or product oriented, focusing on your end users and their customer experiences provides a competitive edge. It sets you apart. It sets you apart because what you're doing suddenly has lasting value in the eyes of the customer.

WOW Moments don't materialize out of thin air. You can't be lazy about it.

You have to be willing to do the work that's required to understand the needs of your end user. Then you can be innovative in developing WOW Moments that truly resonate with each recipient. You can make them fun, rewarding, and meaningful.

When WOW Moments are done correctly, they naturally bring out the core values of your organization and put them front and center for your customers to see. A WOW Moment says, "Our people really care. They care enough to go out of their way for you, the customer."

Remember that the WOW Moment culture starts at the top.

Leadership is, after all, proactive. You can't create an experience from the sidelines or sitting behind a desk. And you can't sell your team on a change in culture if you're not actively living that change. It doesn't work.

The WOW Moment Culture has to be a conscious decision.

As we said earlier, it has to be a culture by design. It has to be well defined and spelled out for everyone in your organization to see. It has to be a culture based upon trust, integrity, and authenticity. It has to be anchored in the customer experience. It has to be part of your everyday work environment. It requires training and practice. But mostly, it requires common sense and the desire to make a difference.

So go ahead. Go the extra mile. Do something special and out of the ordinary. Create a lasting relationship. But more than anything, take an experience and make it extraordinary!

CPSIA information can be obtained
at www.ICGtesting.com
Printed in the USA
LVOW10s0001220318
570664LV00025B/441/P